Spanish
in Three Months

Isabel Cisneros

A DK Publishing Book
www.dk.com

A DK PUBLISHING BOOK

www.dk.com

First American Edition, 1998
10 9 8 7 6 5 4

Published in the United States by
DK Publishing, Inc.
95 Madison Avenue
New York, New York 10016

Copyright © 1998, 1999
Dorling Kindersley Limited, London

Library of Congress Cataloging-in-Publication Data
Spanish in three months.
      p.   cm. -- (Hugo)
      Includes index.
      ISBN 0-7894-3227-7 (alk. paper). -- ISBN 0-7894-3228-5
      (alk. paper with cassette)
      1. Spanish Language--Textbooks for foreign speakers --
      English. I. DK Publishing. Inc. II. Series: Hugo (Series)
      PC 4129.E5S68 1998
      468.2'421 -- dc21   97-47225
                                    CIP

Set in 10/12pt Palatino by
Alastair Wardle
Printed and bound by LegoPrint, Italy

Preface

This updated and enlarged edition of *Spanish in Three Months* has been written for us by Isabel Cisneros, who has considerable experience in teaching her native tongue to high school students, adult beginners, and more advanced students. The book is designed for people working without a teacher, who want to acquire a good working knowledge of Spanish in a short time. The grammar is presented concisely and clearly, maintaining the Hugo principle of teaching only what is really essential – and yet providing a complete course in written and conversational Spanish. Using this book together with the related cassette recordings that we have produced as optional extras will give a further dimension to your studies.

Ideally, you should spend about an hour a day on the course (maybe a little less if you don't use the recordings), although there is no hard and fast rule on this. Do as much as you feel capable of doing. If you have no special aptitude for learning languages, there is no point in forcing yourself beyond your daily capacity to assimilate new material. It is much better to learn a little at a time, and to learn that thoroughly.

In studying the chapters, first read each rule or numbered section carefully and then reread it to ensure that you have fully understood the grammar and examples given. Try to understand rather than memorize; if you have understood, the exercises and drills will ensure that you remember the rules through applying them. Translate the exercises and check your answers against the key at the back of the book. The vocabulary list in each chapter notes those words not previously supplied elsewhere in the text. If you make mistakes and cannot understand why, go back to the relevant grammar section and read it again.

Having completed the written exercises, move on to the drills and speak both stimulus and response out loud. Work through them line by line and use them as a test to see if you are ready to move on to the next chapter. In addition to the valuable oral practice in pronunciation and general fluency provided by these drills, they may also be treated as written exercises. The answers are at the back of the book.

Each chapter ends with a conversation in everyday Spanish, against which you will find an English translation. It is important to remember that idiomatic language cannot be translated word for word without the occasional appearance of some rather formal phrases. These conversations should be read aloud until you can do so without hesitation. Take careful note of the use of idioms and new vocabulary, as well as relating the constructions you hear to those you have just learned.

The course is rounded off with a selection of reading passages taken from modern Spanish literature. You should read these and reread them as soon as you think you can do it without referring to the English translations too often. These will add to your comprehension of the written language passages, and will also give you a taste of the pleasures in store, should you decide to take your study of Spanish to a more advanced level.

When the course is completed, you should have a very good understanding of the language – more than sufficient for general vacation or business purposes, and enough to lead quickly into an exam schedule if this is your eventual goal. Remember that it is important to continue expanding your vocabulary through reading, listening to the radio, if possible, and, best of all, visiting the country. We hope you will enjoy *Spanish in Three Months*, and wish you success with your studies.

Picture Credits
Jacket: all special photography Steve Gorton, Alan Keohane, Neil Lukas, Neil Mersh, and Kim Sayer, except NEIL LUKAS: front cover left.

Contents

Pronunciation

Before you start the first chapter, read the following rules and advice on pronunciation. There's no need to learn these rules by heart; refer back to them at frequent intervals and you will soon know them well. If you use our cassette recordings, everything will be made much clearer. These tapes let you hear the Spanish words and phrases at the same time as you read them. Spanish is a very phonetic language – once you are familiar with its sounds, you will always know how to pronounce the printed word.

Stress

In Spanish, the following rules apply:

a) Most words ending in a **vowel, n,** or **s,** bear the stress on the *next to last* syllable: examen, flores, hombre, cigarrillo.

b) Most words ending in a **consonant** other than **n** or **s,** bear the stress on the *last* syllable: papel, ciudad, mujer, capital.

c) Exceptions to these two rules are indicated by a written accent on the stressed syllable: árbol, lámpara, estación, inglés, música.

d) The written accent is also used to distinguish words that have the same spelling but different meanings: el (the), él (he); si (if), sí (yes); mi (my), mí (me); mas (but), más (more).

e) The vowels **a, e,** and **o** are strong vowels; **i** and **u** are weak ones.

When two strong vowels come together, they are pronounced separately: p*a*ella, te*a*tro, po*e*ta.
When two weak vowels come together, the stress is on the last one: cu*i*da, vi*u*da.
When a strong vowel and a weak one come together, the strong vowel is stressed unless the weak one is accentuated: *a*ire, j*a*ula, o*í*do, a*ú*n.

In our "imitated pronunciation" (see page 12), we show which is the stressed syllable by marking ' in front of it.

Pronunciation of vowels

The Spanish vowels are **a**, **e**, **i**, **o**, and **u**. Each vowel has only one sound. This is not quite so long and broad as the English equivalent given below. The vowel sounds are also short-ened, as they are in other languages, when they occur in an unstressed word or syllable, or preceding a consonant.

a is pronounced like "ah" in English: **al** (to), **la** (the), **casa** (house).
e is pronounced like "ay": **me** (me), **de** (from), **le** (him).
i is pronounced like "ee": **mi** (my), **primero** (first).
o is pronounced like "o": **lo** (the), **no** (no), **gato** (cat).
u is pronounced like "oo": **tu** (your), **su** (their), **uno** (one).

Pronunciation of consonants

There are only two Spanish consonants that are pronounced quite unlike their English counterparts: **z** and **j**. There are others that differ in various lesser ways. Note the following points:

z is pronounced like "th" in "month" or "thick": **voz, luz, paz, vez, zapato**.

j is pronounced like the German guttural "ch," as in "auch," or like "ch" in the Scottish "loch." This sound is merely the English "h" pronounced in the throat: if you find it hard to make, simply pronounce it like an aspirated "h": **ojo, jugar, juzgar, caja**.

ch is pronounced as in "cheap" or "much": **muchacha**.

c before **e** or **i** is pronounced like the Spanish z: **cena, cinco, once**.

g before **e** or **i** is pronounced like the Spanish j: **coger, general, gigante**.

g before any other letter is like "g" in "go": **gato**.

gu before **e** or **i** is like "g" in "go;" before any other vowel it is like "gw" or "goo": **guerra, guía**.

h is not pronounced at all: **hijo, hablar**.

ll is pronounced nearly like "ll" in "million": **calle, silla, llamar**.

ñ is almost like "ni" in "companion": **niño, señor**.

qu is like "k": **que, quince**.

r is rolled on the tip of the tongue more than in English, especially at the beginning of a word or syllable: **raro**.

s is always pronounced sharp, as in "see" or "last," never like a z as in "easy" or "miser": **casa, mesa**.

y is like "y" in "yes": **yo**. But alone or at the end of a word it is like the vowel **i** ("ee"): **y, soy**.

Varying pronunciations

The lisping pronunciation of z, and of c before e or i, is usual in Castile. Since Castilian is considered the best Spanish, we recommend that you adopt this pronunciation in preference to any other variations you may hear. But in Central and South America (and in some parts of Spain), it is usual to pronounce z, and c before e or i, like the English "s."

Many Spaniards pronounce the final d like "th" in "thin," "myth;" some will pronounce d in the middle of a word like "th" in "then." You should avoid copying this; remember to pronounce madre as "mah-dray," not as "mah-thray." A final d should not be made too sharp or distinct.

It is also not unusual for Spaniards to confuse the sound of b with that of v, so that vaca sounds like "baca," etc. This is not wrong, and the tape recordings of this course will illustrate it throughout – see page 37.

The letter ll is pronounced in several ways. We imitate it as l'y, but in some areas of Spain and in Latin America it has a strong guttural sound, with the "l" virtually disappearing. In the Spanish province of Andalusia and in Argentina, it is even stronger, the "l" sound being replaced by something like a soft "j" or the "si" in "occasion." Thus, mantilla (which we imitate as mahn-'tee-l'yah) becomes mahn-'tee-yah or mahn-'tee-j'yah.

Punctuation signs and accents

Question marks and exclamation marks are placed at both ends of the phrase, the first one being inverted. The diaeresis (¨) is placed over **u** when preceded by **g** to show that the **u** must be pronounced: **agüero.** The tilde (~) is placed over **n** when that letter is to be pronounced like "ni" in "onion": **mañana.** The acute accent (´) is the only one used in Spanish; its use is explained on page 7. It never alters the pronunciation of a letter. It is also used in such words as **cuándo** and **dónde** (when, where), when they actually ask a question: **¿Cuándo llega el buque?** (When does the boat arrive?) but **Me alegro cuando llega el buque** (I am glad when the boat arrives).

The Spanish alphabet

This consists of 29 letters, of which K and W are found only in words taken from other languages. Note the letters CH, LL, and Ñ: in Spanish dictionaries, words beginning with any one of these can be found after C, L, and N. Below, we give the "name" of each letter written according to our system of imitated pronunciation (explained below).

A (ah)	J ('Ho-tah)	R ('airr-ay)
B (bay)	K (kah)	S ('ess-ay)
C (thay)	L ('ell-ay)	T (tay)
CH (chay)	LL ('ell-yay)	U (oo)
D (day)	M ('emm-ay)	V ('oo-vay)
E (ay)	N ('enn-ay)	W ('oo-vay-'do-blay)
F ('eff-ay)	Ñ ('enn-yay)	X ('ay-kiss)
G (Hay)	O (o)	Y (ee-gre-'ay-gah)
H ('ah-chay)	P (pay)	Z ('thay-tah)
I (ee)	Q (koo)	

The "Imitated Pronunciation"

For the first four chapters we give the imitated pronunciation of each new word, in footnotes to the section or vocabulary list in which they first appear. In this imitated pronunciation the Spanish sounds are represented by English syllables. Read it as if each syllable were part of an English word and you should always be understood, especially if you bear in mind the modifications noted below. When reading the imitated pronunciation, remember that:

th   (printed bold face) must be pronounced like "th" in "thin," *never* as in "they."

H   (printed as a capital) is to be pronounced gutturally, like "ch" in the German "auch," or the Scottish "loch".

s   is always like "ss" in "missing," *never* like "s" in "easy."

ah   represents the Spanish **a**; this sounds like "ah," but it is shorter than in "harm," "cast." It is *never* like the "a" in "hat," but remember to keep it short and sharp.

o   resembles the sound of "o" in "not," and even slightly approaches the "aw" in "law." It is not as long as in "go."

Chapter 1

In this first chapter you'll learn some basic but extremely important elements of grammar, such as:

- how to say "the," "a," and "some"
- how to recognize whether a noun is masculine or feminine, and which article to use with each gender
- formation of the plural
- how to say "I," "you," "he," "she," "it," "we," "they"
- the present tense of "**tener**," "to have"
- formation of the negative and interrogative

1 Articles

Articles ("the," "a," etc.) agree in gender and number with the noun to which they relate. Thus, if the noun is masculine and singular, the preceding article must also be masculine singular (indicated by *m.s.* in the paragraphs below, with similar abbreviations for feminine and plural).

The definite article "the" is expressed by:

el (*m.s.*)	**el libro** the book
la (*f.s.*)	**la casa** the house
los (*m.pl.*)	**los libros** the books
las (*f.pl.*)	**las casas** the houses

The indefinite article "a," "an," "some," is expressed by:

un (*m.s.*)	**un libro** a book
una (*f.s.*)	**una casa** a house
unos (*m.pl.*)	**unos libros** (some) books
unas (*f.pl.*)	**unas casas** (some) houses

NOTE: The masculine article is used before a feminine singular noun beginning with **a** or **ha**, if the **a** or **ha** takes the stress:

el agua water
el hambre hunger

IMITATED PRONUNCIATION (1): ell 'lee-bro; lah 'kah-sah; los lee-bros; lahs 'kah-sahs; oon 'lee-bro; 'oo-nah 'kah-sah; 'oo-nos 'lee-bros; 'oo-nahs 'kah-sahs; ell 'ah-goo'ah;
ell 'ahm-bray.

2 Nouns

All nouns are either masculine or feminine. There are no neuter nouns. Most nouns ending in **o** are masculine. Most nouns ending in **a, ión, d, z**, are feminine. There are exceptions however:

la mano (*f.*) hand
el camión (*m.*) truck
el lápiz (*m.*) pencil
el guardia (*m.*) police officer

Several words ending in **a** (of Greek origin) are masculine:

el telegrama telegram
el idioma language
el mapa map

Nouns ending in other letters are of varying genders:

el hombre man
la mujer woman
la leche milk
el color color

IMITATED PRONUNCIATION (2): lah 'mah-no; ell kah-me-'on; ell 'lah-pith; ell goo''ah-de-ah; ell tay-lay-'grah-mah; ell e-de-'o-mah; ell 'mah-pah; ell 'om-bray; lah moo-'Hairr; lah 'lay-chay; ell ko-'lorr.

3 Plural of nouns

The plural of nouns is formed by adding **s** to nouns ending in a vowel, and **es** to nouns ending in a consonant:

hombre (man)   → **hombres** (men)
mujer (woman)   → **mujeres** (women)

The plural of nouns ending in **z** is formed by changing the **z** to **c** and adding **es**:

lápiz (pencil)   → **lápices** (pencils)
luz (light)   → **luces** (lights)

Nouns ending in a consonant and bearing an accent on the last syllable lose that accent when the plural is formed:

camión (lorry)   → **camiones** (lorries)

IMITATED PRONUNCIATION (3): 'om-brace; moo-'Hairr-ace; 'lah-pith-ace; looth; 'looth-ace; kah-me-'on-ace.

Exercise 1

Form the plural of:

1 El libro (book)
2 La casa (house)
3 La mujer (woman)
4 El hombre (man)
5 La calle (street)
6 La flor (flower)
7 El jardín (yard)
8 El coche (car)
9 La capital (capital)
10 La ciudad (city, town)
11 La luz (light)
12 La ley (law)

IMITATED PRONUNCIATION (Ex. 1): 5 'kah-l'yay; 6 florr; 7 Harr-'deen; 8 'ko-chay; 9 kah-pe-'tahl; 10 **the**'oo-'dahd; 12 'lay'e.

Exercise 2

Put the appropriate definite article before the following nouns:

1 ... cigarrillos (*m.*, cigarettes)
2 ... vino (*m.*, wine)
3 ... mesas (*f.*, tables)
4 ... cerveza (*f.*, beer)
5 ... pez (*m.*, fish)
6 ... árboles (*m.*, trees)
7 ... padre (*m.*, father)
8 ... madre (*f.*, mother)
9 ... lápiz (*m.*, pencil)
10 ... estaciones (*f.*, stations)
11 ... billete (*m.*, ticket)
12 ... tren (*m.*, train)

Repeat the above exercise using the indefinite article

IMITATED PRONUNCIATION (Ex. 2): **the**-gar-'rree-l'yos;
'vee-no; 'may-sahs; **th**airr-'vay-**th**ah; peth; 'arr-bol-ace; 'pah-dray;
'mah-dray; 'lah-pith; ess-tah-**the**-'on-ace; be-l''yay-tay; trren.

Exercise 3

Translate:

1 the book	7 a city
2 the table	8 some cigarettes
3 the tickets	9 the yard
4 some trees	10 a street
5 a beer	11 some women
6 the car	12 the station

4 Subject pronouns

singular

yo	I
tú	you (*fam.*)
él, ella	he, she
usted	you (*pol.*)

plural

nosotros (*m.*), **nosotras** (*f.*)	we
vosotros (*m.*), **vosotras** (*f.*)	you (*fam.*)
ellos (*m.*), **ellas** (*f.*)	they
ustedes	you (*pol.*)

The forms **tú** and **vosotros/as** (familiar forms) are used to address members of the family, friends, children, and animals. The forms **usted** and **ustedes** (polite forms) are used to address all other people. Usually written as **Vd.** and **Vds.**, or **Ud./Uds.**, they must always be used with the 3rd person of the verb. **Usted** is a contraction of the archaic form of address **Vuestra Merced**, "your honor." Although the familiar form is becoming increasingly common in Spain, it is still advisable to use the polite form when addressing strangers or people you have just met.

Except for **usted** and **ustedes** (which are nearly always expressed), all other subject pronouns are omitted unless emphasis is required or ambiguity must be avoided.

IMITATED PRONUNCIATION (4): yo; too; ell; 'ell-yah; oos-'ted; nos-'otros; nos-'o-trahs; vos-'o-tros; vos-'o-trahs; 'ell-yos; 'ell-yahs; oos-'tay-dace.

5 Other forms of address

The titles **señor** (sir/Mr.), **señora** (madam/Mrs.) and **señorita** (Miss) are used to address people whose name is not known or in front of the person's surname. **Señorita** can also be used in front of the person's Christian name. These titles are always preceded by the definite article except when the person is addressed directly. They are usually written as: **Sr.**, **Sra.**, **Srta.**

¿Un café, señor?	Coffee, sir?
El Sr. Martínez.	Mr. Martínez.
La Sra. Martínez.	Mrs. Martínez.
La Srta. Martínez.	Miss Martínez.
Por aquí, Sr. Martínez.	This way, Mr. Martínez.

The titles **Don** and **Doña**, for which there are no equivalents in English, are used in front of the person's Christian name. Thus: **Don Juan; Doña María.**

IMITATED PRONUNCIATION (5): say-n''yorr; say-n''yor-rah; say-n'yor-'ree-tah; kah-'fay; marr-'tee-neth; porr ah-'kee; don Hoo''ahn; 'don-yah mah-'rree-ah.

6 The verb "tener" (to have, to possess)

This is an irregular verb, and one of the most important in the language, so learn it thoroughly.

Present tense

tengo	I have
tienes	you have
tiene	he, she has, you have (*polite form*)
tenemos	we have
tenéis	you have
tienen	they have, you have (*polite form*)

Tienen una hija. They have a daughter.
Tenemos un coche. We have a car.

IMITATED PRONUNCIATION (6): tay-'nairr; 'ten-go; te-'ay-nace; te-'ay-nay; tay-'nay-mos; tay-'nay-iss; te-'ay-nen; 'ee-Hah.

7 Negative form

The negative is formed by putting the word **no** in front of the verb:

No tengo dinero. I don't have any money.
No tienen cerveza. They don't have any beer.

8 Interrogative form

A sentence is made interrogative by putting the subject after the verb:

Vd. tiene una pluma. You have a pen.
¿Tiene Vd. una pluma? Do you have a pen?

The interrogative is also indicated by intonation in the voice and the use of an inverted question mark at the beginning of a written question.

9 Idiomatic uses of "tener"

There are a number of idioms with **tener** followed by a noun where English usually has "to be" followed by an adjective. Here are some examples:

tener ... años	to be ... years old
tener calor	to be hot
tener cuidado	to be careful
tener en cuenta	to bear in mind
tener éxito	to be successful
tener frío	to be cold
tener ganas de	to feel like, to be interested in

tener gracia	to be funny
tener hambre	to be hungry
tener miedo	to be afraid
tener paciencia	to be patient
tener prisa	to be in a hurry
tener que hacer	to have things to do
tener que ver con	to have to do with
tener razón	to be right
tener sed	to be thirsty
tener sueño	to be sleepy
tener suerte	to be lucky

When **tener que** is followed by an infinitive, it translates "to have to," "must":

Tengo que salir. I have to go out.
Tenemos que ver la iglesia. We must see the church.

IMITATED PRONUNCIATION (9): 'ah-n'yos; kah-'lor; koo'ee-'dah-do; en koo-'en-tah; 'ex-e-to; 'free-o; 'gah-nas day; 'grah-**the**-ah; 'ahm-bray; mee-'ay-do; pah-**the**-'en-**the**-ah; 'pree-sah: kay ah-'**th**airr; kay vairr kon; rrah-'**th**on; sayd; soo''ay-n'yo; soo''air-tay; tay-'nairr kay; sah-'leerr; vairr; e-'glay-se-ah.

As you go through the chapters, your vocabulary will steadily be increased by the introduction of new words in the sentences that illustrate grammar explanations. Additional vocabulary lists like the one below, where new words are shown in the order you will come upon them in the following exercise, should be learned before you begin the written translation work. If you find a word repeated, and you've learned it already, don't worry!

Vocabulary

el café	coffee
trabajar	to work
todo	everything
salir	to go out
el hijo	son

IMITATED PRONUNCIATION: kah-'fay; trah-bah-'Harr; 'to-do; sah-'leerr; 'ee-Ho.

Exercise 4

Translate:

1 They have a house.
2 We don't have any coffee.
3 The man is afraid. *miedo*
4 I have to work.
5 Do you have *(fam. sing.)* a pencil?
6 They are not thirsty. *sed*
7 Do you have *(pol. pl.)* everything?
8 I am hot.
9 We have to go out.
10 He has a son.

Drill

*In this and similar drills that follow, first read the example
that shows both a "stimulus" and a "response" (not necessarily
a simple question and answer). The model will show you how to
tackle the rest of that drill. Thus, in the following, you will see
that the stimulus requires a response alternating between the
first persons singular and plural.*

1 ¿Tiene Vd. una pluma?   Do you have a pen?
No, no tengo una pluma.   No, I don't have a pen.

¿Tienen Vds. un lápiz?   Do you *(pl.)* have a pencil?
No, no tenemos un lápiz.   No, we don't have a pencil.

1 ¿Tiene Vd. hambre?
2 ¿Tienen Vds. cerveza?
3 ¿Tiene Vd. sed?
4 ¿Tienen Vds. calor?
5 ¿Tiene Vd. frío?
6 ¿Tienen Vds. los libros?
7 ¿Tiene Vd. cigarrillos?
8 ¿Tienen Vds. los billetes?

CONVERSATIONS

a)

Sr.	**¿Tiene Vd. una cerveza muy fría? Tengo sed.** *Do you have a very cold beer? I am thirsty.*
Sra.	**Sí, señor. Aquí tiene.** *Yes, sir. Here you are.*
Sr.	**¿Cuánto es?** *How much is it?*
Sra.	**Cincuenta pesetas.** *Fifty pesetas.*
Sr.	**Sólo tengo un billete de mil. ¿Tiene Vd. cambio?** *I only have a one thousand peseta note. Do you have change?*
Sra.	**Sí, señor.** *Yes, Sir.*
Sr.	**Gracias. Adiós.** *Thank you. Good-bye.*

b)

Sra.	**Carmen y Luis tienen un piso en la ciudad y una casa en el campo.** *Carmen and Luis have an apartment in town and a house in the country.*
Sr.	**¿Tiene la casa un jardín grande?** *Does the house have a large yard?*
Sra.	**Sí, muy grande y muy bonito, con árboles y flores. También tienen un perro y un gato.** *Yes, very big and very pretty, with trees and flowers. They also have a dog and a cat.*

Chapter 2

Continuing with the basic essentials, you'll now learn:

- *how to express possession "of"*
- *some common adjectives, and how they must agree in gender and number with the noun to which they are attached*
- *the difference between "**ser**" and "**estar**", both meaning "to be"*
- *how to use these important verbs*

10 Contraction of article

When the prepositions **a** (to) and **de** (of, from) are followed by the definite article **el**, they contract into **al** and **del**, respectively: **al castillo** (to the castle), **del jardín** (from the yard).

11 Possession

There is no possessive case in Spanish. Possession must be expressed by the preposition **de**:

El padre de Juan. John's father (*lit*. The father of John).
El paraguas de la mujer. The woman's umbrella.

IMITATED PRONUNCIATION (10/11): ah, day; ahl kahs-'teel-l'yo; dayl Harr-'deen; 'pah-dray; pah-'rrah-goo'ahs.

Exercise 5

Translate: _a la iglesia_

1 to the church.   7 of the man. _del hombre_
2 of the language. _del idioma_   8 of the city. _de la ciudad_
3 to the car. _al coche_   9 to the street _a la calle_
4 to the table. _a la mesa_   10 of the wine. _del vino_
5 of the trees. _de los arboles_   11 to the police officer. _al policia_
6 to the house.   12 of the station. _de la estacion_
a la casa

12 Adjectives

Adjectives agree in gender and number with the nouns they qualify and generally follow the noun. Adjectives ending in **o** in the masculine change the **o** to **a** in the feminine. The plural is formed by adding **s** to both genders:

El coche blanco. The white car.
La casa blanca. The white house.
Los coches blancos. The white cars.
Las casas blancas. The white houses.

Adjectives ending in **e**, and most adjectives ending in a consonant, have the same form for both masculine and feminine. The plural is formed by adding **s** to those ending in **e**, and **es** to those ending in a consonant. For example:

El lápiz verde. The green pencil.
La pared verde. The green wall.
Los lápices verdes. The green pencils.
Las paredes verdes. The green walls.
Un ejercicio fácil. An easy exercise.
Una lección fácil. An easy lesson.
Unos ejercicios fáciles. Some easy exercises.
Unas lecciones fáciles. Some easy lessons.

Exceptions to this rule are:

a) adjectives of nationality

inglés English (*m.*)
inglesa English (*f.*)
español Spanish (*m.*)
española Spanish (*f.*)

· b) certain adjectives ending in **n** and **or**

holgazán lazy (*m.*)
holgazana lazy (*f.*)
trabajador hardworking (*m.*)
trabajadora hardworking (*f.*)

IMITATED PRONUNCIATION (12): 'blahn-ko; 'blahn-kah;
'blahn-kos; 'blahn-kahs; 'vairr-day; pah-'reth; 'vairr-dace;
pah-'reth-ace; ay-Hairr-'thee-the-o; 'fah-thil; leck-the-'on;
ay-Hairr-'thee-the-os; 'fah-thil-ace; leck-the-'on-ace; in-'gless;
in-'gless-ah; es-pah-'n'yol; es-pah-'n'yo-lah; ol-gah-'thahn;
ol-gah-'thahn-ah; trah-bah-Hah-'dorr; trah-bah-Hah-'dor-rah.

Vocabulary

el periódico	newspaper
la revista	magazine
interesante	interesting
encantador	charming
bueno	good
útil	useful
barato	cheap
largo	long
alto	tall
alemán	German

IMITATED PRONUNCIATION: pay-rre-'o-de-ko; rray-'viss-tah;
in-tay-ress-'an-tay; en-kahn-tah-'dorr; boo''ay-no; 'oo-til;
bah-'rah-to; 'lar-go; 'ahl-to; ah-lay-'mahn.

Exercise 6

Make the following adjectives agree where necessary:
1 Unos hombres bueno.s
2 Una mujer encantadorA
3 Unos libros útil≥s
4 Unas flores blanco. s
5 Un coche barato.
6 Una calle largo.
7 Unos árboles alto.s
8 Unas ciudades interesante. s
9 Un periódico inglés.
10 Una revista alemánA

13 "Ser" and "estar"

It is important to distinguish between the verbs **ser** and **estar**, both of which translate the English "to be."

Present tenses

ser	estar	
soy	**estoy**	I am
eres	**estás**	you are
es	**está**	he/she is, you are (*pol.*)
somos	**estamos**	we are
sois	**estáis**	you are
son	**están**	they are, you are (*pol.*)

IMITATED PRONUNCIATION (13): sairr; es-'tahrr; soy; 'eh-ress; ess; 'so-mos; 'so'ees; son; es-'toy; es-'tahs; es-'tah; es-'tah-mos; es-'tah'ees; es-'tahn.

14 Uses of "ser"

Ser expresses an inherent characteristic or permanent state and it is used to indicate:

a) Identity
   Soy Carmen. I am Carmen.

b) Possession
   El perro es de Juan. The dog is John's.

c) Origin
   Mis amigos son de Madrid.
   My friends are from Madrid.

d) Nationality
   Somos norte americanos. We are American.

e) Occupation
   El padre de María es arquitecto.
   Maria's father is an architect.

f) Material of which something is made
   El reloj es de oro. The watch is made of gold.

g) Inherent characteristics
   Carlos es muy alto. Charles is very tall.

h) Expressions of time
   Son las cinco. It is five o'clock.
   Hoy es lunes. Today is Monday.

i) Impersonal expressions
   Es mejor esperar. It is better to wait.
   Es difícil aprender. It is difficult to learn.

Ser is also used with the past participle of the verb to form the passive voice (see section 82 for further notes on the passive):

El ladrón es apresado por la policía.
   The thief is captured by the police.

IMITATED PRONUNCIATION (14): 'pairr-o; mees ah-'mee-gos; mah-'dreeth; arr-ke-'teck-to; rray-'loH; 'o-ro; moo'e; 'thin-ko; oy'e; 'loo-ness; may-'Horr; ess-pay-'rahrr; de-'fee-thil; ah-pren-'dairr; lah-'dron; ah-pray-'sah-do; po-le-'thee-ah.

15 Uses of "estar"

Estar is used to indicate:

a) Temporary states or conditions
Pedro está enfermo. Peter is ill.

b) Position (whether temporary or permanent)
Carmen está en el salón. Carmen is in the lounge.
Valencia está en España. Valencia is in Spain.

Estar is also used with the present participle of the verb to form the continuous tenses:

Los niños están jugando en el jardín.
The children are playing in the yard.

Estar with the preposition **para** translates "to be about to":

El tren está para llegar. The train is about to arrive.

These basic rules, however, do not cover every situation. There are cases where it is difficult for the student to decide which verb is the right one. For instance, it can be argued that to be young (**joven**) or to be rich (**rico**) is a temporary condition, but in both cases **ser** is used. In the following exercise an English translation will help you decide whether each sentence is "temporary" or "permanent."

IMITATED PRONUNCIATION (15): en-'fairr-mo; sah-'lonn; vah-'len-the-ah; ess-'pah-n'yah; 'nee-n'yos; Hoo-'gahn-do; 'pah-rrah; l'yay-'garr; 'Ho-ven; 'rree-ko.

Exercise 7

Write down these sentences in Spanish, with the appropriate form of "ser" or "estar" where we have omitted them.

1 Las lecciones ... difíciles. *son* — The lessons are difficult.
2 El café ... frío. *está* — The coffee is cold.
3 Las chicas ... alemanas. *son* — The girls are German.
4 Jaime ... muy inteligente. *es* — James is very intelligent.
5 Los libros ... sobre la mesa. *están* — The books are on the table.
6 Ana ... triste. *está* — Ann is sad.
7 La mujer de Luis ... secretaria. *es* — Luis's wife is a secretary.
8 La casa ... pequeña. *es* — The house is small.
9 El coche no ... en el garaje. *está* — The car is not in the garage.
10 Yo ... contento con el hotel. *estoy* — I am pleased with the hotel.

Vocabulary

italiano	Italian
la manzana	apple
en	in
la cocina	kitchen
el autobús	bus
allí	there
la capital	capital
España	Spain
la colina	hill
peligroso	dangerous
fumar	to smoke
demasiado	too much
dulce	sweet
mañana	tomorrow
domingo	Sunday
la playa	beach

IMITATED PRONUNCIATION (Ex. 7/Vocab): 'chee-kahs;
'so-bray; 'triss-tay; say-kray-'tah-ree-ah; pay-'kay-n'yah;
gah-'rrah-Hay; con-'ten-to; con; ee-tah-lee-'ah-no; mahn-'thah-nah;
en; ko-'thee-nah; ah'oo-to-'booss; ah-'l'yee; kah-pe-'tahl;
ess-'pahn-yah; ko-'lee-nah; pay-le-'gro-so; foo-'mahrr;
day-mah-se-'ah-do; dool-thay; mah-'n'yah-nah; do-'meen-go;
'plah-yah.

Exercise 8

Translate:

1 She is Italian. *Ella es italian*
2 The apples are in the kitchen. *Las manzana estan en el cocino*
3 The bus is over there. *El autobus esta allí*
4 Madrid is the capital of Spain. *Madrid es la capital del España*
5 The girl is tall. *La niña es alto*
6 The house is on the hill. *La casa esten la colina*
7 It is dangerous to smoke. *Es peligrosa fumar*
8 The coffee is too sweet. *El cafe esta demasiado dulce*
9 Tomorrow is Sunday. *Mañana es domingo*
10 They are on the beach. *Estan en la playa*

CONVERSATIONS

a)

Juan ¿Dónde está tu padre?
Where is your father?

Teresa Está en el jardín, tomando el sol y leyendo el periódico.
He is in the yard sunbathing and reading the paper.

Juan Y tu madre ¿dónde está?
And your mother, where is she?

Teresa Está en la cocina haciendo una paella para la comida.
She is in the kitchen making a "paella" for lunch.

Juan ¡Una paella! ¡Qué bien!
"Paella!" How lovely!

b)

Recepcionista ¿Es Vd. el señor García?
Are you Mr. García?

Sr. García Sí.
Yes.

Recepcionista Tengo un telegrama para Vd.
I have a telegram for you.

Sr. García ¿De dónde es el telegrama?
Where is the telegram from?

Recepcionista Es de Los Angeles.
It's from Los Angeles.

Sr. García Ah! Muchas gracias.
Oh! Thank you.

Recepcionista De nada.
Not at all.

Chapter 3

> *This chapter includes the following grammar:*
>
> - *demonstrative adjectives and pronouns ("this," "that," "these," "those")*
> - *present tense of regular verbs ending in "-ar," "-er," "-ir"*
> - *use of the present participle*
> - *interrogative pronouns ("what?," "who?," "whose?,"etc.)*
> - *relative pronouns ("who," "which," "that," "of whom," etc.)*

16 Demonstrative adjectives

	Masculine	*Feminine*
this	**este**	**esta**
that	**ese**	**esa**
that (over there)	**aquel**	**aquella**
these	**estos**	**estas**
those	**esos**	**esas**
those (over there)	**aquellos**	**aquellas**

Demonstrative adjectives always precede the noun and agree with it in gender and number:

Este coche. This car.
Esa iglesia. That church.
Aquellos niños. Those children (over there).

A demonstrative adjective cannot be used before one noun and understood (but omitted) before another. It must be repeated:

Estos niños y estas niñas. These boys and girls.
Esas mesas y esas sillas. Those tables and chairs.

Vocabulary

caro	expensive
fuerte	strong
muy	very
viejo	old
el amigo	friend
ocupado	occupied, taken, busy
libre	free
el ascensor	elevator
lleno	full
la uva	grape
agrio	sour

IMITATED PRONUNCIATION (16/Vocab): 'es-tay; 'ay-say;
ah-'kel; 'es-tos; 'ay-sos; ah-'kell-yos; 'es-tah; 'ay-sah; ah-'kell-yah; 'es-
tahs; 'ay-sahs; ah-'kell-yahs; 'kah-ro; foo''air-tay; 'moo'e;
ve-'ay-Ho; ah-'mee-go; o-koo-'pah-do; 'lee-bray; ahs-**then**-'sor;
'l'yay-no; 'oo-vah; 'ah-gre-o.

Exercise 9

Translate:

1 That car is expensive.
2 Those cigarettes are strong.
3 That church is very old.
4 These friends are from Malaga.
5 This table is taken.
6 That man is free.
7 This elevator is full.
8 Those grapes are sour.
9 Those books (over there) are interesting.
10 It is that beach (over there).

1⁊ Demonstrative pronouns

These have the same forms as the adjectives but usually take an accent on the stressed syllable. They agree in gender and number with the noun they replace. For example:

No es este libro, es aquél.
It isn't this book, it's that one over there.
Estos zapatos son caros, ésos son baratos.
These shoes are expensive, those are cheap.

The neuter forms of the pronoun **esto** (this) and **eso, aquello** (that), are used to refer to things the gender of which has not been established. These forms have no plural.

¿Qué es esto? What is this?
Eso no es correcto. That is not correct.

Éste and **aquél**, with their related forms, translate the English "the latter" and "the former" respectively:

Tienen un hijo y una hija. Ésta es enfermera aquél es médico.
They have a son and daughter. The latter is a nurse, the former is a doctor.

Vocabulary	
la maleta	suitcase
la galleta	biscuit
el pan	bread
el abrigo	coat
el zapato	shoe
el vino	wine
la habitación	room

IMITATED PRONUNCIATION: mah-'lay-tah; gahl-'yay-tah; pahn; ah-'bree-go; **th**ah-'pah-to; 'vee-no; ah-be-tah-**th**e-'on.

Exercise 10

Replace the words in parentheses by the correct form of the demonstrative adjective or pronoun:

1 No son (these) libros, son (those ones).
2 No es (that) maleta, es (that one over there).
3 No son (these) galletas, son (those ones).
4 No es (that) pan, es (this one).
5 No es (this) abrigo, es (that one over there).
6 No son (those) zapatos, son (these ones).
7 No es (this) vino, es (that one).
8 No es (that) periódico, es (this one).
9 No son (these) habitaciones, son (those ones).
10 No es (this) coche, es (that one over there).

18 Regular verbs

The infinitive of every Spanish verb ends in **ar**, **er**, or **ir** (habl**ar**, com**er**, viv**ir**). The part preceding these endings is called the stem. Most tenses are formed by adding certain personal endings to the stem. These endings are shown in bold letters, below:

Present tenses

hablar (to speak)	**comer** (to eat)	**vivir** (to live)
habl**o**	com**o**	viv**o**
habl**as**	com**es**	viv**es**
habl**a**	com**e**	viv**e**
habl**amos**	com**emos**	viv**imos**
habl**áis**	com**éis**	viv**ís**
habl**an**	com**en**	viv**en**

No hablo ruso. I don't speak Russian.
¿Habla Vd. español? Do you speak Spanish?
Come mucho pan. He eats a lot of bread.

No comen en el hotel. They don't eat in the hotel.
¿Viven Vds. aquí? Do you live here?
Vivo en Boston. I live in Boston.

Vocabulary

comprar	to buy
beber	to drink
escribir	to write
estudiar	to study
aprender	to learn
subir	to go up, to bring up

IMITATED PRONUNCIATION (18/Vocab): ah-'blahrr; 'ah-blo; 'ah-blahs; 'ah-blah; ah-'blah-mos; ah-'blah-ees; 'ah-blahn; ko-'mairr; 'ko-mo; 'ko-mes; 'ko-may; ko-'may-mos; ko-'may-ees; 'ko-men; ve-'veerr; 'vee-vo; 'vee-ves; 'vee-vay; ve-'vee-mos; ve-'vees; 'vee-ven; 'rroo-so; 'moo-cho; 'lon-dress; kom-'prahrr; bay-'bairr; ess-kre-'beerr; ess-too-de-'ahrr; ah-pren-'dairr; soo-'beerr.

*In listening to the recording of **vivir** in particular, students will have noticed the tendency towards pronouncing "v" as "b." This is what you'll hear more often than not in Spain, and – as we point out in the introductory paragraph dealing with varying pronunciations – it is quite acceptable and not incorrect. However, throughout the printed text we have imitated the Spanish "v" with an English "v."*

Exercise 11

Translate:

1 I buy.
2 He smokes.
3 You (*pol.s.*) drink.
4 We write.
5 They learn.
6 I study.
7 You (*fam.s.*) speak.
8 She eats.
9 We live.
10 They go up.
11 I learn.
12 He drinks.

Exercise 12

Translate:

1 He buys a newspaper.
2 Does she drink beer?
3 Pedro lives in Barcelona.
4 I write to Conchita.
5 Do you study English?
6 These children learn Spanish.
7 He eats too much.
8 We go up the hill.
9 I speak English.
10 They smoke cheap cigarettes.

19 Present participle

The present participle of regular verbs is formed by adding
-ando to the stem of verbs in **ar**, and **-iendo** to the stem of
verbs in **er** and **ir**. For example:

hablar → **hablando** (speaking)
comer → **comiendo** (eating)
vivir → **viviendo** (living)

The present participle used with the present tense of the
verb **estar** forms the present continuous tense ("I am
speaking," "I am eating," "I am living," etc.):

Present continuous

hablar	**comer**	**vivir**
estoy hablando	estoy comiendo	estoy viviendo
estás hablando	estás comiendo	estás viviendo
está hablando	está comiendo	está viviendo
estamos hablando	estamos comiendo	estamos viviendo
estáis hablando	estáis comiendo	estáis viviendo
están hablando	están comiendo	están viviendo

Ramón está bebiendo vino. Ramón is drinking wine.
El gato está subiendo al árbol. The cat is going up the tree.
Estoy aprendiendo francés. I am learning French.

This tense has a more restricted use in Spanish than in
English. It generally indicates an action taking place at the
time of speaking.

IMITATED PRONUNCIATION (19): ah-'blahn-do; ko-me-'en-do;
vee-ve-'en-do; rrah-'mon; bay-be-'en-do; 'gah-to; soo-be-'en-do;
ah-pren-de-'en-do; frahn-'thess.

20 Interrogative pronouns

¿Qué? What?
¿Quién? ¿Quiénes? *(pl.)* Who? Whom?
¿De quién? Whose?
¿Cuál? ¿Cuáles? *(pl.)* Which? What?

¿Qué come Vd.? What do you eat?
¿Quién es Vd.? Who are you?
¿De quién es esta pluma? Whose is this pen?

¿Cuál de estos trenes va a Valencia?
  Which of these trains goes to Valencia?
¿Cuál es su nombre?
  What is your name?

¿Qué? can sometimes play the role of an adjective:

¿Qué libros desea Vd.? Which books do you want?

IMITATED PRONUNCIATION (20): kay; ke-'en; ke-'en-ess;
day ke-'en; koo''ahl; koo''ahl-ess.

21 Relative pronouns

a) **que** (who, which, that).
This can refer to persons or things, singular or plural,
subject or object. Preceded by a preposition, **que** refers only
to things. For example:

La chica que cuida a los niños.
  The girl who looks after the children.

El coche que conduce.
  The car he drives.

La casa en que vivimos.
  The house in which we live.

b) **quien, quienes** (who, whom).
This refers only to persons, subject or object, and is used mainly after prepositions. It is also used after parts of the verb "to be" and a noun or pronoun. For example:

El profesor con quien estudio.
The teacher with whom I study.

El hombre para quien trabaja.
The man for whom he works.

Es él quien tiene la culpa.
It is he who is to blame.

Es María quien tiene que escribir.
It is Maria who has to write.

c) **el que, la que, los que, las que**, and **el cual, la cual, los cuales, las cuales** (who, whom, which, that).
These can refer to persons or things, subject or object, and are generally used after prepositions:

La mujer con la que está hablando.
The woman with whom he is speaking.

El autobús en el que viajo.
The bus in which I travel.

Los amigos de los cuales hablábamos.
The friends of whom we were talking.

el que, la que, los que, las que also translate "he who," "she who," "those who," or "the one/ones who":

El que acaba de llegar es su hijo.
The one who has just arrived is his son.

Los que han venido son todos estudiantes.
Those who have come are all students.

d) **cuyo, cuya, cuyos, cuyas** (whose, of whom, of which).
This is a relative adjective and agrees with the noun it
qualifies:

El hombre cuya hija es actriz.
The man whose daughter is an actress.

La novela cuyo título no recuerdo.
The novel whose title I don't remember.

e) **lo que /lo cual** (what, which) refers to a clause or an idea:

No comprendo lo que dice.
I don't understand what he says.

No ha llegado todavía, lo cual me sorprende.
He hasn't arrived yet, which surprises me.

Note that the relative pronoun can <u>never</u> be omitted in
Spanish (as it often is in English):

El hombre a quien quiero ver. The man I want to see.

El periódico que lee. The newspaper he reads.

IMITATED PRONUNCIATION (21): kay; koo''ee-dah;
kon-'doo-thay; ke-'en: ke-'en-ess; pro-fay-'sorr; 'kool-pah; el kay,
el koo''ahl *etc*; ve''ah-Ho; ah-'kah-bah; ess-too-de-'ahn-tess;
'koo-yah *etc*. ac-'treeth; no-'vay-lah; 'tee-too-lo; rray-koo''air-do;
lo kay; lo koo''ahl; 'dee-thay; to-dah-'vee-ah; sorr-'pren-day;
ke-'ay-ro vairr; 'lay-ay.

Vocabulary

el pueblo	village
la tienda	store
leer (leyendo)	to read (reading)
el médico	doctor
la carta	letter
verde	green
la puerta	door
la pluma	pen
con	with
el número	number

IMITATED PRONUNCIATION: poo''ay-blo; te-'en-dah; lay-'airr; lay-'en-do; 'may-de-ko; 'kahrr-tah; 'vairr-day; poo''air-tah; 'ploo-mah; kon; 'noo-may-ro.

Exercise 13

Translate:

1 The village in which we live.
2 The woman who works in the store.
3 The book that I have to read.
4 The town of which we are speaking.
5 It is Pedro who is (a) doctor.
6 Whose letters are these?
7 Which magazine is he buying?
8 The house that has a green door.
9 The pen with which I write.
10 What is the number?

Drills

2 ¿Son Vds. norte americanos?   Are you (pl.) American?
Sí, somos norte americanos.   Yes, we're American.

¿Es Vd. norte americana?   Are you American?
Sí, soy norte americana.   Yes, I'm American.

1 ¿Beben Vds. cerveza?
2 ¿Come Vd. pan?
3 ¿Viven Vds. en Boston?
4 ¿Es Vd. médico?
5 ¿Hablan Vds. español?
6 ¿Compra Vd. la revista?

3 ¿Es Vd. norte americano?   Are you American?
No, no soy norte americano.   No, I'm not American.

¿Son Vds. norte americanos?   Are you (pl.) American?
No, no somos norte americanos.   No, we're not American.

1 ¿Vive Vd. en Barcelona?
2 ¿Fuman Vds.?
3 ¿Aprende Vd. alemán?
4 ¿Compran Vds. los periódicos?
5 ¿Bebe Vd. vino?
6 ¿Son Vds. españoles?

4 *Replace the blanks by the correct form of the present continuous:*
¿Qué come? Está comiendo pan.

1 ¿Qué compra? … . el periódico.
2 ¿Qué beben? … . cerveza.
3 ¿Qué estudia Vd.? … . español.
4 ¿Qué comen Vds.? … . uvas.
5 ¿Qué lee? … . una revista.
6 ¿Qué fuma Vd.? … . un cigarrillo.
7 ¿Qué hablan Vds.? … . inglés.
8 ¿Qué escribe? … . una carta.
9 ¿Qué aprenden? … . español.
10 ¿Qué sube Vd.? … . las maletas.

CONVERSATION

En la librería
At the bookstore

Dependienta **¿Buenos días, señor. ¿Qué desea?**
Good morning, sir. Can I help you?

Cliente **Buenos días. ¿Tiene Vd. un libro de historia de España?**
Good morning. Do you have a book on the history of Spain?

Dependienta **Sí, señor, tenemos varios. Este es muy bueno, tiene muchas ilustraciones.**
Yes sir, we have several. This one is very good, it has many illustrations.

Cliente **Sí, parece muy interesante. ¿Cuánto es?**
Yes, it looks very interesting. How much is it?

Dependienta **Ochocientas pesetas.**
Eight hundred pesetas.

Cliente **Es un poco caro. Y ése ¿cuánto es?**
It is a little expensive. And that one, how much is it?

Dependienta **Ese, quinientas.**
That one, five hundred.

Cliente **Muy bien, ése por favor.**
All right, that one please.

Chapter 4

Chapter 4 introduces you to expressions of time, together with dates, months, seasons, and days of the week. You will also learn about:

- *possessive adjectives ("my," "your," "his," etc.) and how they agree with the thing possessed, not the possessor*
- *possessive pronouns ("mine," "yours," etc.)*
- *cardinal numbers*
- *ordinal numbers*

22 Possessive adjectives

	singular	*plural*
my	**mi**	**mis**
your	**tu**	**tus**
his, her, its, your (*pol.*)	**su**	**sus**
our	**nuestro (-a)**	**nuestros (-as)**
your	**vuestro (-a)**	**vuestros (-as)**
their, your (*pol.*)	**su**	**sus**

Possessive adjectives agree with the thing possessed, not with the possessor:

Mi coche. My car.
Mis hermanos. My brothers.
Nuestro perro. Our dog.
Nuestras hijas. Our daughters.

Although "his," "her," "its," "their," and "your" are all translated by the forms **su** and **sus**, the meaning is usually clear from the context. However, in cases of ambiguity, the following forms can be used: **de él, de ella, de ellos, de ellas, de Vd., de Vds**. For example:

El libro de Vd. Your book.
El amigo de ellos. Their friend.

Vocabulary

el hermano	brother
la hermana	sister
el tío	uncle
la tía	aunt
el marido	husband
la mujer	wife
el primo	cousin *(m.)*
la prima	cousin *(f.)*
el sobrino	nephew
la sobrina	niece
los padres	parents
los parientes	relatives

IMITATED PRONUNCIATION (22/Vocab): me; mees; too; toos; soo; sooss, etc; airr-'mahn-o; airr-'mahn-ah; 'tee-o; 'tee-ah; mah-'ree-do; moo-'Hairr; 'pree-mo; 'pree-mah; so-'bree-no; so-'bree-nah; 'pah-drace; pah-re-'en-tace.

Exercise 14

Translate:

1 My husband.
2 Her brother.
3 Our sister.
4 Their nephew.
5 His uncle.
6 My parents.
7 Your wife.
8 Their sons.
9 Your (*pol.s.*) cousin (*m.*).
10 His relatives.

---

23 Possessive pronouns

	singular	*plural*
mine	el mío, la mía	los míos, las mías
yours	el tuyo, la tuya	los tuyos, las tuyas
his, hers, its, yours (*pol.*)	el suyo, la suya	los suyos, las suyas
ours	el nuestro, la nuestra	los nuestros, las nuestras
yours	el vuestro, la vuestra	los vuestros, las vuestras
theirs, yours (*pol.*)	el suyo, la suya	los suyos, las suyas

Possessive pronouns agree in gender and number with the noun they replace. They are always preceded by the definite article, except after the verb **ser** when the article is usually omitted. For example:

Mi casa y la tuya. My house and yours.
Estas cartas son nuestras. These letters are ours.

These forms are also used as adjectives, after the noun and without the article –

a) for emphasis:
¿Cuál es el coche vuestro?
  Which is <u>your</u> car?

b) for direct address (as in letters):
Muy señor mío.
  Dear Sir.

c) to translate "of mine," "of yours," etc.:
Un amigo mío.
  A friend of mine.
Una idea suya.
  An idea of his.

IMITATED PRONUNCIATION (23): 'me'o; me 'ah; 'me-os; 'me-ahs; 'too-yo, etc; 'soo-yo, etc.

Exercise 15

Replace the word in brackets with the appropriate form of the possessive pronoun:

 1 Mi casa y (yours, *fam.s.*)
 2 Nuestro jardín y (theirs).
 3 Su coche y (ours).
 4 Mi mujer y (his).
 5 Vuestra madre y (ours).
 6 Su padre y (mine).
 7 Mi cerveza y (yours, *pol.*).
 8 Nuestros amigos y (yours, *fam.pl.*).
 9 Su secretaria y (mine).
10 Tu gato y (hers).

24 Cardinal numbers

1	uno (*m.*), una (*f.*)	50	cincuenta
2	dos	60	sesenta
3	tres	70	setenta
4	cuatro	80	ochenta
5	cinco	90	noventa
6	seis	100	cien, ciento
7	siete	101	ciento uno (-a)
8	ocho	102	ciento dos
9	nueve	200	doscientos (-as)
10	diez	300	trescientos (-as)
11	once	400	cuatrocientos (-as)
12	doce	500	quinientos (-as)
13	trece	600	seiscientos (-as)
14	catorce	700	setecientos (-as)
15	quince	800	ochocientos (-as)
16	dieciséis	900	novecientos (-as)
17	diecisiete	1,000	mil
18	dieciocho	1,001	mil uno (-a)
19	diecinueve	1,002	mil dos
20	veinte	1,100	mil cien
21	veintiuno(-a)	1,101	mil ciento uno (-a)
22	veintidós	1,200	mil doscientos (-as)
23	veintitrés, etc	2,000	dos mil
30	treinta	100,000	cien mil
31	treinta y uno (-a)	200,000	doscientos mil
32	treinta y dos	1,000,000	un millón
40	cuarenta	2,000,000	dos millones

IMITATED PRONUNCIATION: 'oo-no; 'oo-nah; doss; tress; koo''ah-tro; 'thin-ko; 'say-iss; se-'ay-tay; 'o-cho; noo''ay-vay; de- 'eth; 'on-thay; 'do-thay; 'tray-thay; kah-'torr-thay; 'kin-thay; de-'eth-e-'say-iss, etc; (20) 'vay'n-tay; 'vay'n-te-'oo-no, etc; (30) 'tray-in-tah, etc; (40) koo'ah-'ren-tah; thin-koo''en-tah; say-'sen-tah; say-'ten-tah; o-'chen-tah; no-'ven-tah; the-'en; the-'en-to, etc; (1000) meel; (1,000,000) mee-'l'yon.

Uno and **ciento** are contracted to **un** and **cien** in front of a noun or an adjective:

un libro one book
cien libros a hundred books

Exercise 16

Translate:
1 Ten houses.
2 Seventy-two pesetas.
3 Two hundred cigarettes.
4 Sixteen letters.
5 One hundred and thirty-five books.
6 Forty-six hotels.
7 Three hundred and fifty-four apples.
8 Sixty-eight stores.
9 One thousand four hundred men.
10 Seven hundred and eighty-five cars.

---

25 Ordinal numbers

1st **primero**	6th **sexto**
2nd **segundo**	7th **séptimo**
3rd **tercero**	8th **octavo**
4th **cuarto**	9th **noveno**
5th **quinto**	10th **décimo**

Beyond the "tenth," cardinal numbers are generally used:

Felipe II (segundo). Philip II.
Alfonso XII (doce). Alfonso XII.
El siglo III (tercero). The third century.

El siglo XX (veinte). The twentieth century.
El octavo piso. The eighth floor.
El piso trece. The thirteenth floor.

Note that with titles and centuries both ordinal and cardinal numbers follow the noun.

All the ordinal numbers form their feminine and plural in the usual way:

La tercera vez. The third time.
Los primeros días. The first days.

Primero and tercero are shortened to **primer** and **tercer** in front of the masculine noun:

El primer hombre. The first man.
El tercer niño. The third child.

IMITATED PRONUNCIATION (25): pre-'may-ro; say-'goon-do; tairr-'thay-ro; koo''ar-to; 'keen-to; 'sex-to; 'sep-te-mo; ock-'tah-vo; no-'vay-no; 'day-**the**-mo; fay-'lee-pay; ahl-'fon-so; 'see-glo; 'pee-so; veth; 'dee-ahss; pree-'mairr; tairr-'thairr.

Exercise 17

Translate:
1 The seventh book.
2 The first wife.
3 The third daughter.
4 The sixth cigarette.
5 The second door.
6 The tenth day.
7 The fourth street.
8 The ninth child.
9 The fifth man.
10 The eighth store.

26 The time

Telling time is quite easy, as the following examples show:

¿Qué hora es? What is the time?
Es la una. It is one o'clock.
Son las dos. It is two o'clock.
Son las tres. It is three o'clock.

Notice that the feminine article is used because it stands for the unsaid **hora**, and the plural form (in verb as well as article) applies in all hours except one.

"Quarter to" is expressed by **menos cuarto**, "quarter after" by **y cuarto**, and "half past" by **y media**. For example:

Son las siete y diez. It is ten after seven.
Es la una menos veinte. It is twenty to one.
Son las ocho y media. It is 8:30.
Son las cinco menos cuarto. It is quarter of five.
Son las nueve y cuarto. It is quarter after nine.

Mediodía is "midday" and **medianoche** is "midnight." If you want to be exact, **a las once en punto** means "at eleven o'clock precisely." **A eso de** means "at about ... ."

"AM" is expressed by **de la mañana** and "PM" by **de la tarde** or **de la noche** (use the latter for the times after 8:30 PM). For example:

El tren sale a las nueve de la mañana.
 The train leaves at 9 AM

En España comemos a eso de las tres de la tarde.
 In Spain we have lunch at about 3 PM

Pedro llega a su casa a las once de la noche.
 Peter arrives at his house at 11 PM

The expressions **por la mañana** ("in the morning"), **por la tarde** ("in the afternoon," "in the evening"), and **por la noche** ("at night") are used when the time of day is not given:

Ramón trabaja por la mañana.
Ramon works in the morning.
Leo en el jardín por la tarde.
I read in the yard in the afternoon.
Por la noche todo está en silencio.
At night everything is silent.

IMITATED PRONUNCIATION (26): kay 'o-rah ess; 'may-nos koo''ar-to; ee 'may-de-ah; may-de-o-'dee-ah; may-de-ah-'no-chay; mah-n''yah-nah; 'tarr-day; 'no-chay.

27 Days of the week, time expressions

The days of the week (which in Spanish do not begin with a capital letter) are:

lunes	Monday
martes	Tuesday
miércoles	Wednesday
jueves	Thursday
viernes	Friday
sábado	Saturday
domingo	Sunday

The days of the week are always preceded by the definite article **el**. For example:

El domingo por la mañana.
Sunday morning.

Some useful expressions of time:

ayer	yesterday
anteayer	the day before yesterday
hoy	today
hoy día	nowadays
mañana	tomorrow
pasado mañana	the day after tomorrow
mañana por la mañana	tomorrow morning
mañana por la tarde	tomorrow afternoon/evening
mañana por la noche	tomorrow night
de día	by day
de noche	by night
al día siguiente	on the following day
un día sí y otro no	every other day
a los pocos días	a few days later
hace unos días	a few days ago

IMITATED PRONUNCIATION (27): 'loo-ness; 'mar-tess;
me-'air-co-less; Hoo-'ay-vess; ve-'air-ness; 'sah-bah-do;
do-'min-go; ah-'yair; ahn-tay-ah-'yair; 'o'e; 'o'e 'dee-ah;
mah-n''yah-nah; pah-'sah-do; 'no-chay; se-ghee-'en-tay.

28 Months of the year

The months of the year, which are also spelled with a small
initial letter in Spanish, are:

enero	January	julio	July
febrero	February	agosto	August
marzo	March	septiembre	September
abril	April	octubre	October
mayo	May	noviembre	November
junio	June	diciembre	December

29 Seasons of the year

The seasons of the year are:

la primavera	spring	**el otoño**	fall
el verano	summer	**el invierno**	winter

The Spanish seasons are never spelled with a capital initial, as sometimes is the case in English.

IMITATED PRONUNCIATION (28/29): ay-'nay-ro; fay-'bray-ro; 'mar-**th**o; ah-'bril; 'mah-yo; 'Hoo-ne-o; 'Hoo-le-o; ah-'gos-to; sep-te-'em-bray; ok-'too-bray; no-ve-'em-bray; dee-**th**e-'em-bray; pre-mah-'vay-rah; vay-'rah-no; o-'to-n'yo; in-ve-'air-no.

30 Dates

The date can be expressed in two different ways:

a) with the verb **estar**
¿A cuántos estamos?
  What is the date?

b) with the verb **ser**
¿Qué fecha es hoy?
  What is the date today?
Estamos a siete *or* **Es el siete.**
  It's the seventh.

The ordinal number is used for the first of the month, the cardinal numbers for the rest:

El primero de mayo.
  May 1st.

El quince de octubre.
   October 15th.
[Nació] el cuatro de abril de mil novecientos dos.
   [He was born on] April 4th, 1902.

Vocabulary

hasta	until
frío	cold
las vacaciones	vacations
el cumpleaños	birthday
generalmente	usually
ir	to go
cenar	to have dinner
el reloj	watch, clock

IMITATED PRONUNCIATION (30/Vocab): 'fay-chah; nah-**the**-'o;
'ahs-tah; 'frec-o; vah-kah-**the**-'o-ness; koom-play-'ah-n'yos;
Hay-nay-rahl-'men-tay; eer; **th**ay-'narr; rray-'loH.

Exercise 18

Translate:

1 What is the time?
2 It is twenty after ten on my watch.
3 I work until 11:30.
4 The winter in Madrid is cold.
5 They have their vacations in July.
6 My birthday is (on) January 3rd.
7 He is free on Saturdays.
8 October is usually a beautiful month.
9 We have to go to Barcelona in May.
10 On Sundays I have dinner with my parents.

CONVERSATION

Juan y Carmen trabajan en la misma oficina
John and Carmen work in the same office

Juan Oye, Carmen, el sábado doy una pequeña fiesta en mi casa.
Listen, Carmen, on Saturday I am giving a little party at home.

Carmen ¡Ah, qué bien!
How nice!

Juan Es mi cumpleaños y quiero celebrarlo.
It's my birthday and I want to celebrate.

Carmen Así que tu cumpleaños es en junio. El mío también. ¡Qué casualidad!
So, your birthday is in June. Mine too. What a coincidence!

Juan ¿En qué fecha es el tuyo?
What date is yours?

Carmen El dieciocho.
The eighteenth.

Juan Tres días después del mío, entonces. Bueno, ¿puedes venir a mi fiesta?
Three days after mine, then. Well, can you come to my party?

Carmen ¿A qué hora es?
At what time?

Juan A las ocho.
At eight o'clock.

Carmen Me gustaría, pero el sábado tengo que trabajar horas extraordinarias hasta las nueve y media.
I'd like to, but on Saturday I have to work overtime until 9:30.

Juan   **No te preocupes porque la fiesta dura hasta la una o las dos de la mañana.**
Don't worry because the party goes on until one or two in the morning.

Carmen   **En ese caso acepto. ¿Has invitado a mucha gente?**
In that case, I accept. Have you invited many people?

Juan   **No, doce o catorce amigos, porque mi casa no es muy grande. ¿Puedes traer unos discos? Yo tengo solamente unos pocos.**
No, twelve or fourteen friends, because my house is not very big. Can you bring some records? I only have a few.

Carmen   **Sí, con mucho gusto.**
Yes, with pleasure.

Juan   **Hasta el sábado, entonces.**
Until Saturday then.

Carmen   **Adiós y gracias por invitarme.**
Good-bye and thank you for inviting me.

Revision – 1

Exercise 1

Fill in the blanks, choosing a verb from the column on the right:

1 Sólo _____ un billete de mil.	habla
2 Carmen y Pedro _____ en Barcelona.	aprende
3 Mi hermana _____ secretaria.	son
4 ¿Dónde _____ los periódicos?	cena
5 Los niños no _____ mucho pan.	viven
6 Es italiano pero _____ español.	trabajamos
7 Estos zapatos _____ muy caros.	es
8 Ramón _____ generalmente a las nueve.	están
9 Mi primo _____ francés y alemán.	comen
10 Nosotros no _____ los sábados.	tengo

Exercise 2

Translate:

1 In Spain, American newspapers are very expensive.
2 Where are the suitcases?
3 The room is on the third floor.
4 In the summer they live in the United States and in the winter they live in Spain.
5 Her husband is sick, he drinks too much.
6 I have to write to my German friend (*f.*).
7 These flowers are for John's mother.
8 Mrs. Suarez is a charming woman.
9 We have to buy the tickets.
10 What is the time? Quarter after seven.
11 Is that dog yours (*pol.*)?
12 Our daughter is learning Spanish.

Exercise 3

Answer the following questions by translating the sentences shown in English:

1   ¿De dónde eres?
    I am American.

2   ¿Entonces vives en New York?
    No, I live in Delaware.

3   ¿Por qué estás en España?
    I am on vacation.

4   ¿Cuántas semanas de vacaciones tienes?
    Only two.

5   ¿Trabajas?
    Yes, I work in a store.

6   ¿Qué clase de tienda?
    It's a bookstore.

7   ¿Estás en un hotel?
    No, I am at a friend's (f.) house.

8   ¿Dónde vive tu amiga?
    In a house on the beach.

9   ¿Tienes sed? ¿Quieres (would you like) una cerveza?
    No, thank you, I am in a hurry. Good-bye.

Chapter 5

In this chapter, we cover the past participle and the perfect tense (which introduces "**haber**" "to have").
Other topics include:

- the verb "**ir**," "to go"
- how to translate "there is" and "there are"
- personal pronouns used with direct and indirect objects ("me," "to me," "you," "to you," etc.)
- the imperative mood

31 The verb "ir" (to go)

This is an irregular verb. Its present tense is as follows:

voy	**vamos**
vas	**vais**
va	**van**

Ir a translates "to go to" and "to be going to," e.g.:

Van a la iglesia.
   They go to church.
Voy a comprar un periódico.
   I am going to buy a newspaper.

The 1st person plural **vamos** translates "let's" as well as "we go to" and "we are going to." The meaning is usually clear from the context:

Vamos al cine todos los viernes.
   We go to the movies every Friday.
Vamos a comprar los billetes.
   We are going to buy the tickets.
Vamos a ver.
   Let's see.

Vocabulary

ir de vacaciones	to go on vacation
por	by
tomar	to have (food or drink)
cantar	to sing
descansar	to rest
ir de compras	to go shopping
el mercado	market
el teatro	theater

Exercise 19

Translate:

1 We go to church on Sundays.
2 I am going to buy that book.
3 He goes to his friend's house.
4 We go on vacation in the summer.
5 They go to Madrid by train.
6 Let's have coffee.
7 She is not going to sing.
8 Tomorrow I am going to rest.
9 They go shopping in the market.
10 Let's go to the theater.

32 The past participle

The past participle of regular verbs is formed by adding **-ado** to verbs ending in **-ar**, and **-ido** to verbs ending in **-er** and **-ir**.

hablar	→ **hablado** (spoken)
comer	→ **comido** (eaten)
vivir	→ **vivido** (lived)

There are some irregular past participles. Here are a few examples:

escribir (to write)	→ **escrito** (written)
ver (to see)	→ **visto** (seen)
hacer (to do, to make)	→ **hecho** (done, made)
decir (to say, to tell)	→ **dicho** (said, told)

33 The perfect tense

This tense is formed with the present indicative of **haber** (to have) followed by the past participle of the appropriate verb. For example, the perfect tense of the verb **comprar** (to buy) is:

he comprado	I have bought
has comprado	you have bought
ha comprado	he has bought
hemos comprado	we have bought
habéis comprado	you have bought
han comprado	they have bought

Haber is an auxiliary verb and is never used as a synonym of **tener**.

The use of the perfect tense in Spanish is similar to that in English:

Hemos viajado todo el día.
   We have traveled all day.

Note that the auxiliary and the past participle must not be separated in Spanish:

Siempre he trabajado.
   I have always worked.

34 "hay"

"There is" and "there are" are rendered by **hay,** which is an impersonal form of the verb **haber.** Note that **hay** has no plural:

Hay una barca en la playa.
   There is a boat on the beach.
Hay muchos turistas en esta ciudad.
   There are many tourists in this town.

Hay que followed by an infinitive is usually translated by "one must":

Hay que ver la catedral.
   One must see the cathedral.
No hay que llorar.
   One must not cry.

"There has been" and "there have been" are rendered by the 3rd person singular of the perfect tense of the verb **haber (ha habido):**

Ha habido un accidente de carretera.
There has been a road accident.

Ha habido muchos problemas.
There have been many problems.

Vocabulary

el azúcar	sugar
el té	tea
nuevo	new
el vestido	dress
terminar	to finish
el trabajo	job, work
ayudar	to help
la naranja	orange
la bolsa	bag
la película	film

Exercise 20

Translate:

1 I have written three letters.
2 They have spoken in Spanish.
3 We have eaten too much.
4 There is sugar in this tea.
5 She has bought a new dress.
6 Have you finished the job?
7 He has never helped in the house.
8 There are some oranges in the bag.
9 Have you (*pol.sing.*) drunk the beer?
10 I haven't seen the movie.

35 Personal "a"

All verbs except **tener** must be followed by the preposition **a** when the direct object is a definite person or animal:

Llamo a Pedro. I call Peter.
Llamo a mi perro. I call my dog.
but ...
Tiene un perro. He has a dog.
Compra el libro. He buys the book.

Vocabulary

visitar	to visit
llamar	to call
preparar	to prepare
la comida	meal, food
invitar	to invite
casado (-a)	married
el caballo	horse
bañar	to bathe
esperar	to wait for, to expect
el profesor	teacher

Exercise 21

Rewrite the following sentences filling in the blanks with the personal "a" where necessary:

1 Voy a ver ... mi tío.
2 Tenemos que ayudar ... nuestros amigos.
3 Juan ha comprado ... un perro.
4 No he hablado ... el médico.
5 Está leyendo ... el periódico.   →

6 Vamos a invitar ... Pedro.
7 Tengo ... tres hermanos.
8 Esperamos ... una carta de María.
9 Voy a beber ... una cerveza.
10 Están llamando ... su hija.

Exercise 22

Translate:

1 He visits his mother.
2 I have seen the woman.
3 We have to call the children.
4 María prepares the meal.
5 They have invited their friends.
6 She has a married sister.
7 I am going to buy a horse.
8 We have to bathe the dog.
9 They are waiting for the teacher.
10 Carlos has not seen Toledo.

36 Personal pronouns – direct and indirect object

Direct object

me	me
te	you (*fam.*)
le	him, you (*pol.m.*)
la	her, you (*pol.f.*)
lo, la	it (*m.*), it (*f.*)
nos	us
os	you (*fam.*)
les	them, you (*pol.m.*)
las	them, you (*pol.f.*)
los, las	them (*m., f.*) *referring to things*

Indirect object

me	to me
te	to you
le	to him, to her, to it, to you (*pol.*)
nos	to us
os	to you
les	to them, to you (*pol.*)

Object pronouns usually precede the verb:

Nos ayuda con el trabajo. He helps us with the work.
Le he escrito una carta. I have written him a letter.

When the verb is an infinitive, a present participle, or an imperative, the pronoun is usually added to the end of the verb:

Tengo que comprarlo. I have to buy it.
Está esperándome. He is waiting for me.
Bébalo. Drink it.

If the infinitive or present participle is preceded by another verb, as in the above examples, the object pronoun may be placed before that verb:

Lo tengo que comprar. I have to buy it.
Me está esperando. He is waiting for me.

When an object pronoun is added to the present participle, an accent must be used so that the stress still falls on the same syllable:

Está bebiéndolo. He is drinking it.
Estamos terminándolo. We are finishing it.

37 Order of object pronouns

When two object pronouns come together, the indirect object pronoun is always placed first:

Me lo da. He gives it to me.
Nos la lee. He reads it to us.

When two pronouns of the third person come together, the indirect object pronoun **le/les** becomes **se:**

Se la envía. He sends it to him.

In order to avoid any possible ambiguity in the meaning of **le**, **les**, or **se**, you may use **a él, a ellas, a Vd.**, etc., after the verb:

Le escribo la carta a él. I write the letter to him.
Les compro flores a ellas. I buy them flowers.
Se lo he dado a Vd. I have given it to you.

37a Redundant use of object pronouns

When, for reasons of emphasis or distinction, a noun or strong pronoun, direct or indirect object, precedes the verb, the corresponding object pronoun must also be used immediately before the verb:

A esos amigos les veo poco.
I don't see much of those friends.

A Juan le he comprado una corbata.
I have bought a tie for Juan.

A nosotros no nos han invitado.
They haven't invited us.

Even when the indirect object noun or strong pronoun follows the verb, the corresponding object pronoun is often inserted, especially in conversation:

Se lo he dicho a Pedro. I have told Pedro.

Vocabulary

ofrecer	to offer
la taza	cup
enviar	to send
la carne	meat
el pescado	fish
comprender	to understand
vender	to sell
la bicicleta	bicycle

Exercise 23

Replace the words in parentheses by the appropriate form of the object pronoun:

1 Juan ofrece (un cigarrillo) (a su amigo).
2 Bebo (una taza de té) por la mañana.
3 Hemos comprado (un coche).
4 Me ha enviado (unas flores).
5 He escrito (una carta) (a mi tía).
6 Comemos (la carne y el pescado).
7 Estos señores no comprenden (el inglés).
8 Tengo que estudiar (la lección).
9 Nos ha vendido (las bicicletas).
10 Hemos dado (los libros) (a Pedro).

38 The imperative mood

a) In regular verbs, the polite imperative is formed by adding the following endings to the stem:

	sing.	*pl.*
	-e	**-en** to verbs ending in -ar
	-a	**-an** to verbs ending in -er and -ir
hablar	**hable Vd.**	**hablen Vds.** (speak)
comer	**coma Vd.**	**coman Vds.** (eat)
subir	**suba Vd.**	**suban Vds.** (go up)

Vd. is usually added to the polite form of the imperative.

Object pronouns are placed after the imperative unless it is negative:

Bébalo Vd. Drink it.
No lo beba Vd. Don't drink it.
Envíeselo Vd. Send it to him.
No se lo envíe Vd. Don't send it to him.

b) In irregular verbs the polite imperative is usually formed by adding the same endings as for regular verbs (above) to the stem of the first person singular of the present indicative:

	Present	*Imperative*
tener (to have)	**tengo**	**tenga Vd./tengan Vds.**
decir (to say)	**digo**	**diga Vd./digan Vds.**
contar (to count)	**cuento**	**cuente Vd./cuenten Vds.**

Note the irregular forms of **ir**: **vaya Vd./vayan Vds.**

Exercise 24

Translate:

1 Don't smoke those cigarettes.
2 Drink this wine.
3 Send me the magazine.
4 Read them the letter.
5 Sell him your watch.
6 Learn these numbers.
7 Write your name here.
8 Don't eat those apples.
9 Don't buy that meat.
10 Don't give them to me.

Repeat the exercise, putting the imperative in the plural.

Drills

5 ¿Ha tomado Vd. el café?   Have you had the coffee?
No, voy a tomarlo ahora.   No, I am going to have it
now.

1 ¿Ha tomado Vd. la cerveza?
2 ¿Han ido de compras?
3 ¿Ha escrito la carta?
4 ¿Han hecho Vds. el trabajo?
5 ¿Ha comprado Vd. los cigarrillos?
6 ¿Han visto a su padre?
7 ¿Han terminado Vds. la comida?
8 ¿Ha llamado a Conchita?
9 ¿Ha subido Vd. las maletas?
10 ¿Han bebido Vds. el vino?

→

6 ¿Preparo la comida?   Should I prepare the meal?
Sí, prepárela.   Yes, prepare it.

¿Preparamos la comida?   Should we prepare the meal?
Sí, prepárenla.   Yes, prepare it.

1 ¿Compro el periódico?
2 ¿Subimos las maletas?
3 ¿Llamo al profesor?
4 ¿Invitamos a esos amigos?
5 ¿Leo la carta?
6 ¿Enviamos estas flores?
7 ¿Bebo esta cerveza?
8 ¿Vendemos esta bicicleta?

7 Beba Vd. el café.   Drink the coffee.
Ya lo he bebido.   I have already drunk it.

Beban Vds. el café.   Drink the coffee.
Ya lo hemos bebido.   We have already drunk it.

1 Prepare Vd. el pescado.
2 Llamen Vds. al perro.
3 Escriba Vd. su nombre.
4 Tomen Vds. la carne.
5 Compre Vd. los billetes.
6 Hablen Vds. a los profesores.
7 Cuente Vd. los libros.
8 Vendan Vds. el reloj.
9 Lea Vd. esta revista.

CONVERSATION

Un día muy ocupado
A very busy day

Carmen ¿Qué vas a hacer hoy?
What are you going to do today?

Antonio Hoy tengo varias cosas que hacer. Primero tengo que ir al banco, y después voy a ir a ver a Carlos que está en el hospital.
Today I have several things to do. First I have to go to the bank, and then I am going to see Charles who is in the hospital.

Carmen ¿En el hospital? ¿Qué le pasa?
In the hospital? What is the matter with him?

Antonio Ha tenido un accidente de automóvil volviendo de Málaga.
He has had a car accident coming back from Málaga.

Carmen Y ¿ha sido muy grave?
And was it very serious?

Antonio No. Tiene una pierna rota y dos o tres heridas leves.
No. He has a broken leg and two or three minor injuries.

Carmen ¡Pobre hombre! Tengo que llamar a su mujer y ofrecerle mi ayuda, si la necesita.
Poor man! I must call his wife and offer my help if she needs it.

Antonio Sí, esa es una buena idea.
Yes, that's a good idea.

Carmen Bueno, y por la tarde ¿qué vas a hacer?
Right, and in the afternoon what are you going to do?

Antonio **Tengo que pasarme por la oficina, pero no voy a estar mucho tiempo.**
I have to call in at the office, but I'm not going to be long.

Carmen **Entonces, ¿podemos ir al cine? Ponen una película francesa en el Roxy que deseo ver. Mi hermana la ha visto y me ha dicho que es muy buena.**
In that case can we go to the movies? They are showing a French movie at the Roxy that I want to see. My sister has seen it and she has told me that it is very good.

Antonio **Pues, te espero a las siete menos cuarto a la puerta del cine. ¿Vale?**
So … I'll wait for you at a quarter to seven outside the theater. All right?

Carmen **Muy bien.**
Fine.

Chapter 6

Here you'll learn about some verbs that change their spelling
in the stem (as well as the ending), and you'll also meet
reflexive verbs for the first time. Plus:

- interrogative and exclamative words
- impersonal verbs
- some irregular present tenses
- the verbs "**gustar**" ("to like") and "**querer**" ("to love,"
  "to want/wish")
- idiomatic uses of "**hacer**," ("to do/make")

39 Some useful interrogative words

¿Dónde? ¿Adónde?	Where? Where (to)?
¿Cómo?	How?
¿Cuándo?	When?
¿Cuánto, -a, -os, -as?	How much? How many?
¿Por qué?	Why?

Note that **porque** written as one word means "because."
¿Verdad? (literally "true") is used to seek corroboration to
a statement:

¿Dónde está la pluma?
  Where is the pen?
¿Adónde van Vds.?
  Where are you going?
¿Cómo está Vd.?
  How are you?

¿Cuándo salimos?
   When are we going out?
¿Cuántos libros necesitas?
   How many books do you need?
¿Por qué no compras el coche?
   Why don't you buy the car?
Porque no tengo dinero.
   Because I have no money.
Conchita es muy simpática, ¿verdad?
   Conchita is very nice, isn't she?

39a Exclamatives

¡Cómo!	What! How … !
¡Cuánto, -a, -os, -as!	How much … ! What a lot … !
¡Qué!	What a … ! How … !
¡Quién!	Would that I … /If only I … !
	(imperfect subjunctive)

¡Cómo pesa esta maleta!
   This suitcase is heavy!
¡Cómo! ¿No vas a venir a la fiesta?
   What! You're not coming to the party?
¡Cuánto tenemos que hablar!
   How much/What a lot we have to talk about!
¡Qué caras son estas manzanas!
   These apples are expensive!
¡Qué bonita iglesia!
   What a lovely church!
¡Qué pena!
   What a pity!
¡Qué amable!
   How kind!
¡Qué asco!
   How revolting!
¡Quién tuviera dinero!
   If only I had money!

Note that if the noun following **Qué** is itself followed by a qualifying adjective, either **tan** or **más** must precede the adjective:

¡Qué casa tan grande!
  What a big house!

¡Qué mujer más trabajadora!
  What a hardworking woman!

¡Qué niños tan traviesos!
  How naughty the children are!

40 Radical-changing verbs

There are several Spanish verbs that change their stem vowels when the stress falls on them: **e** changes to **ie**, **o** changes to **ue**, and in some verbs of the third conjugation **e** changes to **i**.

Present tenses

pensar (to think)	**volver** (to return)	**pedir** (to ask for)
pienso	vuelvo	pido
piensas	vuelves	pides
piensa	vuelve	pide
pensamos	volvemos	pedimos
pensáis	volvéis	pedís
piensan	vuelven	piden

The first and second person plural remain regular since the stem vowel is not stressed. Radical changing verbs will be shown in subsequent vocabularies as follows:

pensar (ie); **volver** (ue); **pedir** (i).

41 Reflexive verbs

When the object of the verb is the same person or thing as its subject, the verb is called reflexive. These are much more common in Spanish than in English.

Reflexive pronouns

me	myself
te	yourself
se	himself, herself, itself, yourself (*pol.*)
nos	ourselves
os	yourselves
se	themselves, yourselves (*pol.pl.*)

The 3rd person of the reflexive pronoun, **se**, is attached to the infinitive of verbs that are reflexive:

lavarse	to wash oneself
sentarse (ie)	to sit down
dormirse (ue)	to go to sleep

Present tense of **lavarse**

me lavo
te lavas
se lava
nos lavamos
os laváis
se lavan

Regarding their position, reflexive pronouns follow the same rules as object pronouns:

Me lavo. I wash myself.
Tengo que lavarme. I have to wash myself.
Estoy lavándome. I am washing myself.
Lávese Vd. Wash yourself.
No se lave Vd. Don't wash yourself.

Some verbs change their meaning when used reflexively:

llamar	to call
llamarse	to call oneself, to be called
ir	to go
irse	to go away
dormir	to sleep
dormirse	to go to sleep
llevar	to carry, to wear
llevarse	to take away

With some verbs the reflexive pronoun may be used to give emphasis or finality to the action of the verb:

decidir, decidirse a	to decide
morir, morirse (ue)	to die
parar, pararse	to stop

42 Reciprocal form

The reflexive pronoun is also used in reciprocal verbs such as:

quererse (ie)	to love each other
comprenderse	to understand each other
verse	to see each other

Mi hermano y yo no nos comprendemos.
My brother and I don't understand each other.

Vocabulary

todos los días	everyday
casarse	to get married
odiar(se)	to hate (each other)
ayudar(se)	to help (each other)
acostarse (ue)	to go to bed

Exercise 25

Translate:

1 Pedro and Anita write to each other every day.
2 The car is going to stop.
3 We are going to get married.
4 The children go to bed at eight o'clock.
5 We have to wash ourselves.
6 The two men hate each other.
7 He always asks me for money.
8 They never help each other.
9 Carlos returns from the office at 6:30.
10 I must go to sleep.
11 Take away these cups!
12 The street is called Baeza.
13 I am going to sit here.
14 We are going away tomorrow.
15 I have decided to live in Spain.

43 Personal pronouns with prepositions (disjunctive)

After prepositions, the same forms as those of the subject pronouns are used, except for:

mí (me); **ti** (you, *familiar*); **sí** (himself, herself, yourself)

Estas cartas son para mí. These letters are for me.
No vuelve con nosotros. He does not come back with us.
Vamos sin ella. We go without her.

With the preposition **con** ("with"), the forms **mí**, **ti**, and **sí** become **conmigo**, **contigo**, and **consigo**:

No puedo vivir contigo.
   I cannot live with you.
Siempre lleva un libro consigo.
   He always carries a book with him(self).

Consigo can only be used reflexively; otherwise, the forms "with him," "with her," "with you," "with them," are translated by **con él, con ella, con Vd.**, etc.

Vocabulary

el regalo	present
para	for
el tiempo	weather
contra	against
sin	without
siempre	always
el viaje	journey
entre	between
según	according to

Exercise 26

Translate:

1 We are working with them.
2 He has bought a present for me.
3 Is he going to come back with you (*pol.s.*)?
4 The weather is against us.
5 They have gone away without him.
6 He has always lived with me.
7 These letters are for her.
8 They are going to buy the house between them.
9 Are the children with you (*fam.s.*)?
10 According to him, the journey is too long.

44 Irregular verbs in the present tense

In their present tenses the following verbs are irregular only in the first person singular:

poner (to put)	**pongo**, pones, pone, ponemos, ponéis, ponen
salir (to go out)	**salgo**, sales, sale, salimos, salís, salen
ver (to see)	**veo**, ves, ve, vemos, veis, ven
hacer (to do, to make)	**hago**, haces, hace, hacemos, hacéis, hacen
traer (to bring)	**traigo**, traes, trae, traemos, traéis, traen
dar (to give)	**doy**, das, da, damos, dais, dan
saber (to know)	**sé**, sabes, sabe, sabemos, sabéis, saben

45 Idiomatic uses of "hacer"

Besides translating "to do," "to make," **hacer** is used:

a) in certain impersonal expressions relating to the weather

¿Qué tiempo hace? What's the weather like?
Hace frío. It's cold.
Hace (mucho) calor. It's (very) hot.
Hace sol. It's sunny.
Hace viento. It's windy.
Hace buen día. It's a nice day.

b) in certain expressions of time

Hace muchos años. Many years ago.
Hace media hora. Half an hour ago.
¿Hace mucho tiempo que esperas?
    Have you been waiting long?

c) in some other idiomatic expressions

hacer(se) daño	to hurt oneself
no hacer caso	to ignore, not to take any notice
hacerse rico	to become rich
hacer señas	to motion
hacerse a algo	to become used to something

46 Impersonal verbs

llover (ue)	to rain
nevar (ie)	to snow
helar (ie)	to freeze
tronar (ue)	to thunder
amanecer	to dawn
anochecer	to get dark

47 The verb "gustar"

This verb translates "to like," "to be keen on," but in the Spanish construction the English subject becomes the indirect object and the English object becomes the subject.

Me gusta el café. I like coffee.
Nos gusta Estados Unidos. We like the United States.
Les gustan las uvas. They like grapes.
A Carlos le gusta pintar. Carlos likes painting.

When the subject of **gustar** is a verb, as in the sentence **A Carlos le gusta pintar,** the infinitive must always be used. Note also that the preposition **a** must be used in front of the noun that is the indirect object.

Sometimes a disjunctive pronoun is used for emphasis or to indicate a contrast. For example:

¿A Vd. le gusta el flamenco?
    Do you like flamenco?
A mí no me gustan los deportes, pero a mi marido le gustan mucho.
    I don't like sports, but my husband likes them very much.

There are other verbs that have the same construction in Spanish as **gustar**:

bastar (to suffice, to be enough)
Este dinero me basta.
    This money is enough for me.

faltar (to be missing, to be short of)
Siempre les falta tiempo.
    They are always short of time.

hacer falta (to need, to be necessary)
Nos hace falta más vino.
    We need more wine.

parecer (to seem, to think (of))
¿Qué te parecen estos pantalones?
    What do you think of these pants?

quedar (to remain, to have left)
¿Le quedan entradas para la función de la tarde?
    Do you have any tickets left for the evening performance?

sobrar (to be/to have more than enough)
Nos sobra tiempo para llegar a la estación.
    We have more than enough time to get to the station.

Exercise 27

Translate:

1 What is the weather like?
2 Today it's very cold.
3 It's going to rain tomorrow.
4 I don't like this beer.
5 He is going to bring us coffee.
6 He likes to go out every evening.
7 I don't know where it is.
8 They go to Spain because they like the sun.
9 Twenty-five years ago.
10 Carmen likes to sit in the yard.

48 The verb "querer" (ie)

This verb means "to love" (a person or animal) or "to want,"
"to wish." It must not be confused with **gustar,** although the
form **quisiera** (imperfect subjunctive) often translates the
English "I should like":

Quiero a mis hijos.
  I love my children.
No quieren ir a Francia.
  They don't want to go to France.
Quisiera ver a Ramón.
  I would like to see Ramón.

Drills

8 ¿Les gusta a Vds. España? Do you like Spain?
Sí, nos gusta mucho. Yes, we like it very much.

1 ¿Le gusta a Vd. la playa?
2 ¿Le gustan a Carlos los deportes?
3 ¿Les gusta a Vds. vivir en Madrid?
4 ¿Os gusta la cerveza?
5 ¿Le gusta a Conchita el regalo?
6 ¿Te gustan los niños?
7 ¿Le gusta a Vd. viajar?
8 ¿Les gusta a tus amigos el vino?
9 ¿Les gusta a Vds. el hotel?
10 ¿Les gusta a ellos el pescado?

9 Van Vds. con Carlos ¿verdad? You are going with Carlos, aren't you?
Sí, vamos con él. Yes, we are going with him.

1 Trabaja Vd. con María ¿verdad?
2 Esta carta es para nosotros ¿verdad?
3 Su hermano vuelve con Vd. ¿verdad?
4 Vamos al teatro sin los niños ¿verdad?
5 Estas flores son para mí ¿verdad?
6 Vive con sus padres ¿verdad?
7 Estos periódicos son para Vds. ¿verdad?
8 Va Vd. de compras sin su marido ¿verdad?

10 ¿Quiere Vd. acostarse? Do you want to go to bed?
Sí, quisiera acostarme. Yes, I would like to go to bed.

¿Quieren Vds. acostarse? Do you want to go to bed?
Sí, quisiéramos acostarnos. Yes, we would like to go to bed.

1 ¿Quiere Vd. sentarse?
2 ¿Quiere Vd. lavarse?
3 ¿Quiere Vd. dormirse?
4 ¿Quiere Vd. irse?
5 ¿Quiere Vd. pararse?
6 ¿Quieren Vds. sentarse?
7 ¿Quieren Vds. lavarse?
8 ¿Quieren Vds. dormirse?
9 ¿Quieren Vds. irse?
10 ¿Quieren Vds. pararse?

CONVERSATION

Planes de vacaciones
Vacation plans

Miguel ¿Adónde van Vds. de vacaciones este año?
Where are you going on vacation this year?

Pilar Vamos a un pueblo de la costa del Mediterráneo, cerca de Valencia.
We are going to a village on the Mediterranean coast, near Valencia.

Miguel ¿En qué mes van Vds.?
Which month do you go?

Pilar Vamos en julio porque hace muy buen tiempo. Hace calor y el mar está delicioso para bañarse.
We go in July because the weather is very good. It's warm and the sea is lovely to bathe in.

Miguel A nosotros nos gusta más el norte. Todos los años vamos a Santander en agosto.
We like the north better. Every year we go to Santander in August.

Pilar Pero en el norte hace mal tiempo, llueve mucho y hay muchos días en los que es imposible ir a la playa.
But in the north the weather is bad, it rains a lot and there are many days when it's impossible to go to the beach.

Miguel Es verdad. Pero no vamos buscando el sol, vamos huyendo del calor de Madrid que en agosto es insoportable.
It's true. But we are not seeking the sun, we are running away from the heat in Madrid which, in August, is unbearable.

Pilar Pues, a mí me gusta el calor. Ya tenemos bastante frío todo el invierno.
Well, I like the hot weather. We are cold enough all through the winter.

Miguel Yo, sin embargo, prefiero el invierno al verano.
I, on the other hand, prefer winter to summer.

Pilar Sobre gustos no hay nada escrito.
There is no accounting for tastes.

Chapter 7

Chapter 7 covers the imperfect and pluperfect tenses, and how to form adverbs (leading to the comparison of adjectives and adverbs).
Learn also:

- some more negative words and expressions
- irregular comparisons
- comparison of nouns (inequality: "more ... than," "fewer ... than," etc.)

49 The imperfect tense

The imperfect is used to express an habitual action, an action repeated over an indefinite period of time, with no beginning or end. It translates the English "was doing," "used to do," sometimes "did" and also "would" in the sense of "used to."

Imperfect tenses

hablar	comer	vivir
hablaba	comía	vivía
hablabas	comías	vivías
hablaba	comía	vivía
hablábamos	comíamos	vivíamos
hablabais	comíais	vivíais
hablaban	comían	vivían

Carlos compraba el periódico todos los días.
Carlos used to buy the newspaper every day.
El hombre vendía caramelos.
The man was selling candy.

As the first and third persons singular have the same forms, the subject pronoun is sometimes used to avoid ambiguity.

There are only three verbs that are irregular in the imperfect tense:

ser (to be)	**ir** (to go)	**ver** (to see)
era	iba	veía
eras	ibas	veías
era	iba	veía
éramos	íbamos	veíamos
erais	ibais	veíais
eran	iban	veían

Íbamos a España una vez al año.
We used to go to Spain once a year.

The forms "there was," "there were," are translated by **había** (the imperfect of the verb **haber**):

Había mucha gente en la playa.
There were a lot of people on the beach.
Había un embotellamiento en la plaza.
There was a traffic jam in the square.

50 The verb "soler"(ue)

This is a defective verb only used in the present and imperfect indicative. It translates "to be in the habit of" and expressions with "generally," "usually," "as a rule":

Suelo levantarme a las siete.
  I usually get up at seven.
Solíamos ir de paseo los domingos.
  We used to go for a walk on Sundays.

51 The pluperfect tense

This is a compound tense and is formed with the imperfect of the auxiliary **haber** and the past participle of the appropriate verb. Thus:

Habíamos comido.
  We had eaten.
Habían escrito.
  They had written.
Ramón había salido.
  Ramón had gone out.

Vocabulary	
el gerente	manager
los bombones	chocolates
el muchacho	boy
buscar	to look for
la representación	performance
empezar (ie)	to begin
la fábrica	factory
el mar	sea
mirar	to look at

Exercise 28

Translate:

1 Luis was smoking a cigarette.
2 I usually see her in the morning.
3 They had spoken to the hotel manager.
4 He used to bring me chocolates.
5 The boy was looking for his suitcase.
6 The performance used to start at ten o'clock.
7 He had worked in a factory.
8 The sea was very cold.
9 The woman was looking at us.
10 We usually ate a lot of fish.

52 Negatives

jamás, nunca	never
nada	nothing
tampoco	neither
nadie	no one, nobody
ninguno (-a)	none
ni ... ni	neither ... nor

Nunca sale de casa.
   He never goes out of the house.
Nadie lo había visto.
   Nobody had seen it.
Ni fuma, ni bebe.
   He neither smokes nor drinks.

However, the double negative is more common in Spanish:

No necesito nada.
   I don't need anything.
Mi padre no lo sabe tampoco.
   My father doesn't know either.

No escribe nunca.
He never writes.

Ninguno (-a) can play the role of adjective or pronoun. It may refer to people or things and it is always used in the singular. As an adjective the masculine form shortens to **ningún** in front of the noun:

No hay ningún niño en la playa.
There aren't any children on the beach.

Voy a comprar cigarrillos, no tengo ninguno.
I am going to buy cigarettes, I don't have any.

Corresponding to these negatives, there are the affirmative forms:

siempre	always
algo	something
también	also, too
alguien	someone, somebody
alguno (-a)	some, any
o ... o	either ... or

Alguno, like its opposite **ninguno**, shortens to **algún** in front of the masculine noun. It may sometimes be used in the singular when a plural form would be usual in English.

Quiero comprar algún periódico norte americano.
I want to buy some American newspapers.

Alguien ha preguntado por Vd.
Somebody has asked for you.

O canta, o baila.
Either he sings or he dances.

Vocabulary

conocer	to know
la leche	milk
venir (ie)	to come
poder	to be able
ocurrir	to happen

Exercise 29

Fill in the blanks with the appropriate negative word:

1 Juan no quiere hacer _____.
2 No conocemos a _____ en esta ciudad.
3 No tienen _____ pan _____ leche.
4 María no viene _____ a verme.
5 No he leído _____ libro de Cervantes.
6 Carlos no puede ir y su hermano _____.
7 _____ sabe lo que ha ocurrido.
8 No hay _____ nuevo.
9 No hemos comprado _____ revista.
10 Esa mujer no ha trabajado _____.

53 Adverbs

Many adverbs are formed in Spanish by adding the ending
-mente to the feminine form of the adjective:

maravillosamente wonderfully
fácilmente easily
frecuentemente frequently

When two or more adverbs ending in **-mente** follow one another, only the last one ends in **-mente**; the others keep the feminine form of the adjective:

El niño ha sido castigado justa y severamente.
The boy has been punished justly and severely.

In using some adverbs, there's an occasional pitfall or special construction to watch out for. Here are some examples.

- **ahora** now

¿Qué vas a hacer ahora?
What are you going to do now?

- **ya** now, already, (no) longer, yet (with an interrogative)

Ya lo veo.
I can see now.

Ya han terminado de comer.
They have already finished eating.

Ya no vivimos en esa casa.
We no longer live in that house.

¿Se ha despertado ya?
Has he woken up yet?

Ya is often used simply for emphasis, and it is not translated in English:

¡Ya lo verás!
You'll see!

¡Ya voy!
I'm coming!

¡Ya lo creo!
I should think so!

● **entonces** then (at that time, in that case)

Yo trabajaba entonces en una compañía de seguros.
I was then working for an insurance company.

¿No quieres venir al cine? Entonces iré yo solo.
Don't you want to come to the movies? Then I'll go
alone/by myself.

● **luego** then (next, soon after, later)

**Primero tenemos que ir al banco y luego a la agencia
de viajes.**
First we have to go to the bank and then to the
travel agent's.

¡Hasta luego!
See you later!

Desde luego.
Of course. Indeed!

Exercise 30

Form adverbs from the following adjectives:
1 feliz (happy).
2 verdadero (true).
3 triste (sad).
4 lento (slow).
5 nuevo (new).
6 agradable (pleasant).
7 malo (bad).
8 cierto (certain).
9 rápido (fast).
10 claro (clear).

54 Comparison of adjectives and adverbs

The comparison of equality "as ... as" is rendered by
tan ... como:

Carlos es tan alto como Pedro.
  Carlos is as tall as Pedro.
Nadie habla tan despacio como Juan.
  Nobody talks as slowly as Juan.

The comparison of inequality ("more ... than," "less ... than")
is rendered by **más ... que, menos ... que**:

Yo soy más pobre que Vd.
  I am poorer than you.
María es menos inteligente que su hermana.
  Maria is less intelligent than her sister.
Mi mujer ha llegado más tarde que yo.
  My wife has arrived later than I.
Este hombre trabaja menos diligentemente que aquél.
  This man works less diligently than that one.

55 Irregular comparison of adjectives

bueno (good)   → **mejor** (better)
malo (bad)   → **peor** (worse)
mucho (a lot of)   → **más** (more)
poco (little, few) → **menos** (less, fewer)
grande (big)   → **mayor** (bigger, older)
pequeño (small)   → **menor** (smaller, younger)

Grande and **pequeño** also have a regular comparison,
más grande and **más pequeño**, which refers only to size:

Esta casa es más grande que la mía.
  This house is bigger than mine.

Mejor, peor, mayor, and **menor** have a plural form ending in **-es,** for masculine and feminine.

56 Irregular comparison of adverbs

bien (well)	→ **mejor** (better)
mal (badly)	→ **peor** (worse)
mucho (much)	→ **más** (more)
poco (little)	→ **menos** (less)

Pilar canta mal, pero yo canto peor que ella.
Pilar sings badly, but I sing worse than she does.

57 Comparison of nouns

The comparison of inequality has the same forms as that of adjectives and adverbs: **más ... que, menos ... que:**

Carmen tiene más paciencia que Pilar.
Carmen has more patience than Pilar.
Tengo menos libros que tú.
I have fewer books than you.

The comparison of equality is expressed by **tanto ... como.**
Tanto is an adjective and has to agree in gender and number with the following noun:

No he bebido tanto vino como Pedro.
I haven't drunk as much wine as Pedro.
Vd. no recibe tantas cartas como yo.
You don't receive as many letters as I do.

Vocabulary

fuerte	strong
el jerez	sherry
seco	dry
negro	black
el zapato	shoe
azul	blue
pronto	soon
necesitar	to need
el agua (*f.*)	water
caliente	hot, warm
la piscina	swimming pool

Exercise 31

Translate:

1 My brother is stronger than I.
2 This sherry is drier than that one.
3 Carlos is three years older than María.
4 The black shoes are smaller than the blue (ones).
5 His car is better than mine.
6 He writes worse than his sister.
7 I have arrived sooner than my father.
8 They haven't as much money as their friends.
9 I don't need as many suitcases as you.
10 The water in the pool is warmer than in the sea.

Drills

11 ¿Iban Vds. al mercado?   Did you go to the market?
Sí, solíamos ir.   Yes, we used to go.

¿Leía Vd. el periódico?   Did you read the paper?
Sí, solía leerlo.   Yes, I used to read it.

1 ¿Veía Vd. a Carmen?
2 ¿Comían en el hotel?
3 ¿Trabajaban Vds.?
4 ¿Escribía Vd. cartas?
5 ¿Viajaba a Londres?
6 ¿Iban Vds. al café?
7 ¿Hablaba Vd. español?
8 ¿Invitaba a sus amigos?
9 ¿Tenían dinero?
10 ¿Bebía Vd. vino?

12 ¿Ha venido alguien?   Has anyone come?
No, no ha venido nadie.   No, nobody has come.

1 ¿Quiere Vd. algo?
2 ¿Han vivido aquí siempre?
3 ¿Quieren Vds. té o café?
4 ¿Hay algún turista inglés?
5 ¿Conocen Vds. a alguien?
6 ¿Tiene Vd. alguna revista española?

13 Mi casa es pequeña.   My house is small.
La mía es más pequeña.   Mine is smaller.

1 Mis libros son viejos.
2 Mi coche es malo.
3 Mi jardín es bonito.
4 Mi hotel es bueno.
5 Mi marido es alto.
6 Mis zapatos son caros.
7 Mis maletas son grandes.
8 Mis cigarrillos son baratos.

CONVERSATION

El Sr. Sánchez habla con su secretaria
Mr. Sánchez speaks with his secretary

Sr. Sánchez Buenos días, Lolita. Llego más tarde que de costumbre.
Good morning, Lolita. I'm later than usual.

Lolita Sí. ¿Qué le ha ocurrido? Son casi las diez.
Yes. What's happened to you? It's almost ten o'clock.

Sr. Sánchez El coche no arrancaba esta mañana. Como ha helado durante la noche, el motor estaba muy frío.
The car wouldn't start this morning. The engine was very cold because it was freezing during the night.

Lolita ¡Qué lata! Por eso yo nunca vengo en el coche. Uso el Metro. Es mucho más rápido y me ahorro muchos problemas.
What a nuisance! That is why I never come in the car. I use the subway. It's much quicker and I save myself a lot of problems.

Sr. Sánchez Claro. Así no tiene Vd. gastos ni de gasolina ni de aparcamiento. Yo creo que voy a hacer lo mismo pronto.
Of course. That way you don't have the expenses of either gas or parking. I think I am going to do the same soon.

Lolita Es lo mejor. No lo dude.
It's the best thing. Believe me.

Sr. Sánchez ¿Ha venido alguien?
Has anyone called?

Lolita   **No. No ha venido nadie.**
No. Nobody has called.

Sr. Sánchez   **Y, ¿hay algún recado?**
And are there any messages?

Lolita   **No, nada. Hay algunas cartas que he dejado en su escritorio.**
No, nothing. There are some letters that I have left on your desk.

Sr. Sánchez   **Bueno. Entonces, voy a ver el correo, y dentro de media hora venga Vd. a mi despacho porque quiero dictarle unas cartas.**
All right. I'm going to see the mail, then; and in half an hour come to my office, because I want to dictate a few letters.

Lolita   **Muy bien, Sr. Sánchez.**
Very well, Mr. Sánchez.

Revision – 2

Drill 1

Do this drill in exactly the same way you've done all the others so far.

¿Qué prefieres, el té o el café? — What do you prefer, tea or coffee?

Me gusta más el café. — I like coffee better/I prefer coffee.

1 ¿Qué prefieren ustedes, el vino o la cerveza?
_____ el vino.

2 ¿Qué preferís, la carne o el pescado?
_____ la carne.

3 ¿Qué prefiere Carlos, el campo o la playa?
_____ la playa.

4 ¿Qué prefieres, el fútbol o el rugby?
_____ el rugby.

5 ¿Qué prefieren los niños, jugar o ver la televisión?
_____ jugar.

6 ¿Qué prefiere usted, Barcelona o Madrid?
_____ Barcelona.

Exercise 1

Translate:

1 I am going to a party tomorrow and I need a new dress.
2 We have seen a very good movie at the "Roxy."
3 He cannot come to the beach with us, he's got too much work.

4 Pedro is very pleasant, but he has no patience with the children.

5 The performance doesn't start till 10:15 P.M. – it's too late for us.

6 They have not been able to go out because it has rained all day.

7 We have to wait until 4:30 P.M. because the stores are closed (cerradas).

8 The English drink more sherry than the Spanish.

Drill 2

Practice your imperatives!

¿Compro el pan?	Should I buy the bread?
Sí, cómprelo./	Yes, buy it.
No, no lo compre.	No, don't buy it.

1 ¿Lavo este vestido?
   Sí, _____.

2 ¿Espero a Carmen?
   No, _____.

3 ¿Pregunto a ese señor?
   Sí, _____.

4 ¿Me llevo las tazas?
   No, _____.

5 ¿Llamo al gerente?
   Sí, _____.

6 ¿Invito a Miguel?
   No, _____.

7 ¿Pongo las flores en agua?
   Sí, _____.

8 ¿Hago el café?
   No, _____.

*When you've done the previous drill, answering **Sí** or **No** as indicated, you can do it again and reverse your replies ... you won't find these alternatives in the Key, but it's all useful extra practice.*

Drill 3

More imperatives!

¿Compramos el pan?   Should we buy the bread?
Sí, cómprenlo./   Yes, buy it.
No, no lo compren.   No, don't buy it.

1   ¿Terminamos el vino?
    Sí, _____.

2   ¿Pedimos el pescado?
    No, _____.

3   ¿Vemos la habitación?
    Sí, _____.

4   ¿Nos bañamos en la piscina?
    No, _____.

5   ¿Compramos unos periódicos?
    Sí, _____.

6   ¿Preparamos la cena?
    No, _____.

7   ¿Enviamos las cartas?
    Sí, _____.

8   ¿Ayudamos a Pedro?
    Sí, _____.

Exercise 2

Complete the sentences given in column A with the correct sentence from Column B:

A
1 Juan está en el hospital … .
2 Queremos ir al cine … .
3 Vienen todos los años a España … .
4 El viernes es su cumpleaños … .
5 Estoy esperando a mi marido … .
6 No han querido bañarse en la piscina … .
7 Vamos a necesitar más dinero … .
8 No me gustan los pueblos de la costa … .

B
a) el agua estaba fría.
b) hay demasiados turistas.
c) ha ido a llamar por teléfono.
d) se ha roto una pierna.
e) si queremos comprar todos esos regalos.
f) les gusta mucho el sol.
g) ponen una película muy buena.
h) va a dar una fiesta en su casa.

Exercise 3

Here is a conversation between you and María about your friend Luisa's birthday. Put your words into Spanish.

Usted	The day after tomorrow is Luisa's birthday.
María	Sí, tenemos que comprarle un regalo.
Usted	What can we buy her?
María	No sé, ¿tienes alguna idea?
Usted	I can only think of chocolates, flowers …
María	No, no. Tiene que ser algo más original.
Usted	She reads a lot and she likes traveling. Why don't we buy her a travel book (libro de viajes)?
María	Bueno, eso es una posibilidad.
Usted	Then we'll go shopping this afternoon and we look for something.
María	¡Vale!

Chapter 8

> Here you'll learn about the future and conditional tenses, and how some irregular verbs change their stem in the future. Other sections cover:
>
> • shortened forms of adjectives
> • adjectives that always precede the noun
> • three irregular present tenses
> • verbs preceded by prepositions

58 Shortening of adjectives

The following adjectives have shortened forms:

a) before the masculine noun

bueno (good)	**buen**
malo (bad)	**mal**
alguno (some)	**algún**
ninguno (none)	**ningún**
primero (first)	**primer**
tercero (third)	**tercer**
uno (one)	**un**

b) before nouns of either gender

grande (big)	**gran**
ciento (100)	**cien**
cualquiera (any)	**cualquier**

Un buen libro. A good book.
Una buena película. A good movie.
El primer tren. The first train.
La primera fila. The first row.
Cualquier autobús. Any bus.
Cualquier persona. Any person.

59 Position of adjectives

Adjectives in Spanish usually follow the noun, but there are some exceptions. Adjectives that *always precede* the noun are:

a) adjectives of quantity

mucho	a lot of
poco	little
tanto	so much
cuanto	how much
demasiado	too much
bastante	enough

b) indefinite adjectives

alguno	some, any
ninguno	none
cada	each
otro	other
todo	all
tal	such

Cada is an invariable word:

Cada hombre y cada mujer.
Each man and each woman.

Otro is never preceded by the indefinite article:

Otro hombre y otra mujer.
Another man and another woman.

Tal is invariable and never followed by the indefinite article:

Tal hombre y tal mujer.
Such a man and such a woman.

c) numerals (cardinal and ordinal) – but see section 25 for exceptions.

d) Some common adjectives like **bueno** (good), **malo** (bad), **pequeño** (small), **hermoso** (beautiful), **joven** (young), and **viejo** (old) often precede the noun:

Un hermoso paisaje. A beautiful landscape.
Un joven guitarrista. A young guitarist.

Certain adjectives change their meaning according to their position:

grande - Una casa grande. A big house.
but - **Una gran mujer.** A great (famous) woman.

nuevo - Un coche nuevo. A (brand) new car.
but - **Un nuevo coche.** A new (different) car.

pobre - Un hombre pobre. A poor (impecunious) man.
but - **Un pobre hombre.** An unfortunate man.

mismo - El mismo hombre. The same man.
but - **El hombre mismo.** The man himself.

In spite of all these rules, the position of adjectives in Spanish is fairly flexible and is often determined by emphasis, balance, and style. Observation and practice will help you overcome any initial difficulties.

Vocabulary

el pintor	painter
llevar	to wear, to carry
la ropa	clothes
la zona	area
perder (ie)	to lose
el bolso	pocketbook
el sombrero	hat
la bebida	drink
el sello	postage stamp
el nadador	swimmer

Exercise 32

Translate:

1 We have had a good journey.
2 Each man had a job.
3 He is a great painter.
4 They always wear the same clothes.
5 There are enough hotels in this area.
6 The poor woman has lost her pocketbook.
7 I have a brand new hat.
8 We have asked for another drink.
9 These stamps are very old.
10 All the children are good swimmers.

60 Present tense of three irregular verbs

venir (to come)	**oír** (to hear)	**decir** (to say, to tell)
vengo	oigo	digo
vienes	oyes	dices
viene	oye	dice
venimos	oímos	decimos
venís	oís	decís
vienen	oyen	dicen

61 Some irregular past participles

(See section 32 for others)

abrir (to open)	→ **abierto**
decir (to say)	→ **dicho**
poner (to put)	→ **puesto**
romper (to break)	→ **roto**
volver (to return)	→ **vuelto**
describir (to describe)	→ **descrito**

62 The future tense

The future tense of regular verbs is formed by adding the following endings to the infinitive: **-é, -ás, -á, -emos, éis, -án**.

hablar (to speak)	**comer** (to eat)	**vivir** (to live)
hablar**é**	comer**é**	vivir**é**
hablar**ás**	comer**ás**	vivir**ás**
hablar**á**	comer**á**	vivir**á**
hablar**emos**	comer**emos**	vivir**emos**
hablar**éis**	comer**éis**	vivir**éis**
hablar**án**	comer**án**	vivir**án**

Hablaremos en español todo el tiempo.
  We will speak Spanish all the time.
Comerá con nosotros mañana.
  He will eat with us tomorrow.
Vivirán cerca de sus padres.
  They will live near his parents.

63 Irregular verbs in the future tense

A few verbs are irregular in the future tense. The endings remain the same as for regular verbs, but the *stem* changes:

caber (to fit in)	cabré, cabrás, etc.
decir (to say)	diré, dirás, etc.
haber (to have)	habré, habrás, etc.
hacer (to do)	haré, harás, etc.
poder (to be able)	podré, podrás, etc.
poner (to put)	pondré, pondrás, etc.
querer (to want)	querré, querrás, etc.
saber (to know)	sabré, sabrás, etc.
salir (to go out)	saldré, saldrás, etc.
tener (to have)	tendré, tendrás, etc.
valer (to be worth)	valdré, valdrás, etc.
venir (to come)	vendré, vendrás, etc.

No podremos ir. We shall not be able to go.
Diré unas pocas palabras. I shall say a few words.
Vendrán con él. They will come with him.

64 The conditional

The conditional is formed by adding the following endings to the infinitive: **-ía, -ías, -ía, -íamos, -íais, -ían**.

hablar	**comer**	**vivir**
hablaría	comería	viviría
hablarías	comerías	vivirías
hablaría	comería	viviría
hablaríamos	comeríamos	viviríamos
hablaríais	comeríais	viviríais
hablarían	comerían	vivirían

As the first and third persons singular have the same forms, the subject pronoun is sometimes used to avoid ambiguity:

Me gustaría ir a la fiesta. I should like to go to the party.
No vivirían en España. They would not live in Spain.

65 Irregular verbs in the conditional

Verbs that are irregular in the future tense are also irregular in the conditional with the same stem change:

decir → di*r*ía; **hacer** → ha*r*ía; **tener** → ten*dr*ía;
venir → ven*dr*ía, etc.

Yo quería saber lo que diría.
  I wanted to know what he would say.
Tendrían que pagar el daño.
  They would have to pay the damage.

66 Other uses of the future and the conditional

The future and the conditional may be used to express probability or assumption:

¿Por qué no ha venido Pedro? Why hasn't Pedro come?
Estará enfermo. He is probably ill.
¿Cuántos años tenía el niño? How old was the boy?
Tendría nueve años. He must have been nine.

"Will" and "would" expressing will or determination are translated by **querer**:

No quiere contestar el teléfono.
He will not answer the phone.
No quería venir con nosotros.
He would not come with us.
¿Quiere Vd. un café?
Will you have coffee?
¿Quiere Vd. cerrar la puerta, por favor?
Will you shut the door, please?

"Should" introducing a suggestion, as in the following examples, is translated by the present tense:

Should we sit down?
¿Nos sentamos?
Should I call the police?
¿Llamo a la policía?

"Should" introducing a moral obligation or recommendation is translated by the conditional form of **deber**:

Deberías decirles la verdad.
You should tell them the truth.
Miguel debería dejar de fumar.
Michael should give up smoking.

Vocabulary

próximo	next
temprano	early
esta noche	tonight
conducir	to drive
andar	to walk
lejos	far
el museo	museum
el autocar	coach

Exercise 33

Translate:

1 They will get married next month.
2 I will go to bed early tonight.
3 He will come with us on vacation.
4 We will visit them on Sunday.
5 They will not speak to us.
6 It would be better to stop.
7 I wouldn't like to drive a big car.
8 He won't have to walk very far.
9 They wouldn't be worth anything.
10 We won't be able to see the museum.
11 He would not sell the house.
12 The coach will leave at eight o'clock.

67 Verbs with prepositions

A verb preceded by a preposition must always be an infinitive:

Le veré antes de salir.
   I'll see him before leaving.
Se ha ido sin hablar con nosotros.
   He has left without speaking to us.

Vocabulary

cerrar (ie)	to close
la ventana	window
antes de	before
después de	after
de	of, from
pasar	to spend (time)
llorar	to cry
sentirse (ie)	to feel
enfermo	ill
el marisco	seafood
la habitación	room
tomar	to take
la voz	voice
ronco (-a)	hoarse
gritar	to shout
enseñar	to show, to teach

Exercise 34

Translate:

1 Close the windows before going to bed.
2 I will have to think before deciding.
3 You cannot go without finishing the job.
4 He has spent the day without speaking to anyone.
5 She was crying without knowing why.
6 They were feeling sick after eating seafood.
7 I was very sleepy after working all night.
8 We would like to see the room before taking it.
9 His voice was hoarse from shouting so much.
10 After writing the letter show it to me.

68 Idiomatic uses of "llevar" and "hacer"

Llevar (to wear, to carry) and **hacer** (to do, to make) are often used to express how long an action has or had been going on:

¿Cuánto tiempo lleva Vd. en España?
  How long have you been in Spain?
Hace tres meses que estoy aquí.
  I have been here three months.
¿Cuánto tiempo llevan Vds. esperando?
  How long have you been waiting?
Hace media hora que esperamos.
  We have been waiting half an hour.

Question and answer can be reversed thus:

¿Cuánto tiempo hace que está Vd. en España?
Llevo tres meses aquí.
¿Cuánto tiempo hace que esperan Vds?
Llevamos media hora esperando.

Drills

14 ¿Ha venido tu amigo? Has your friend come?
No, vendrá luego. No, he will come later.

¿Ha leído Vd. el periódico? Have you read the
newspaper? No, lo leeré luego. No, I will read it later.

1 ¿Han visto a su padre?
2 ¿Han terminado Vds. el trabajo?
3 ¿Ha ido Vd. al banco?
4 ¿Ha escrito Pedro la carta?
5 ¿Han enviado Vds. las flores?
6 ¿Han cerrado la tienda?
7 ¿Ha salido Juan?
8 ¿Ha hecho Vd. la comida?
9 ¿Han visto las habitaciones?
10 ¿Ha abierto Vd. las ventanas?

15 *Study the examples in section 68, then do the following drill:*

1 ¿Cuánto tiempo lleva Vd. estudiando español?
_____ seis meses _____
2 ¿Cuánto tiempo llevan Vds. en Madrid?
_____ tres años _____
3 ¿Cuánto tiempo llevan ellos trabajando aquí?
_____ dos semanas _____
4 ¿Cuánto tiempo lleva Juan viviendo en Detroit?
_____ un año _____
5 ¿Cuánto tiempo lleva Vd. esperando?
_____ diez minutos _____
6 ¿Cuánto tiempo hace que estudia Vd. español?
_____ seis meses _____
7 ¿Cuánto tiempo hace que están Vds. en Madrid?
_____ tres años _____
8 ¿Cuánto tiempo hace que ellos trabajan aquí?
_____ dos semanas _____
9 ¿Cuánto tiempo hace que Juan vive en Detroit?
_____ un año _____
10 ¿Cuánto tiempo hace que espera Vd.?
_____ diez minutos _____

CONVERSATION

Un encuentro en la calle
A chance meeting in the street

Pedro   **Teresa, ¡cuánto tiempo sin vernos!**
Teresa, we haven't met for a long time!

Teresa   **¿Cómo estás?**
How are you?

Pedro   **Muy bien, gracias. Y tú ¿qué haces en Madrid? ¿No vivías en Sevilla?**
Very well, thank you. And you, what are you doing in Madrid? Weren't you living in Seville?

Teresa   **Ya no. Mi marido está trabajando aquí ahora. Llevamos tres meses en Madrid.**
No longer. My husband is working here now. We have been in Madrid three months.

Pedro   **¡Ah, muy bien! ¿Habéis encontrado piso ya?**
Oh, very good! Have you found an apartment yet?

Teresa   **No. De momento estamos viviendo con los padres de Antonio. Pero el piso no es muy grande y estamos un poco apretados.**
No. At the moment we are living with Antonio's parents. But the apartment is not very big and we are a little cramped.

Pedro   **¿Qué tipo de piso buscáis? Porque tengo un amigo que vende uno con tres dormitorios, salón, comedor, cocina y baño. Y también tiene una terraza bastante grande. Lo que no sé es lo que pide. ¿Crees que puede interesarte?**
What sort of apartment are you looking for? Because I have a friend who is selling one with three bedrooms, living room, dining room, kitchen, and bathroom. It also has quite a large balcony. What I don't know is how much he is asking. Do you think it may interest you?

Teresa ¡Ya lo creo! Si el precio es razonable. ¿Cómo podemos ponernos en contacto con él?
Yes, indeed! If the price is reasonable. How can we get in touch with him?

Pedro Se llama Alberto Solís, y estos son su teléfono y sus señas.
His name is Alberto Solís, and this is his phone number and address.

Teresa Pues, muchísimas gracias, Pedro. A ver si tenemos suerte.
Well, thank you very much, Pedro. Let's see if we are lucky.

Pedro Eso espero. Hasta pronto.
I hope so. See you soon.

Teresa Sí. Te llamaremos. Adiós.
Yes. We'll call you. 'Bye.

Chapter 9

In Chapter 9 you'll find out about the past historic tense,
in both regular and irregular verbs, and how this tense
contrasts with the imperfect. Learn also:

* the difference between "**saber**" and "**conocer**"
  (both meaning "to know")
* the superlative of adjectives and adverbs
* other uses of the definite and indefinite articles

69 The past historic

The past historic is used to express a completed action, an
action that took place within a definite period of time.

hablar	comer	vivir
habl**é**	com**í**	viv**í**
habl**aste**	com**iste**	viv**iste**
habl**ó**	com**ió**	viv**ió**
habl**amos**	com**imos**	viv**imos**
habl**asteis**	com**isteis**	viv**isteis**
habl**aron**	com**ieron**	viv**ieron**

Ayer hablé con Carmen.
 Yesterday I spoke to Carmen.
Comieron sopa y pescado.
 They ate soup and fish.
Vivió en Madrid diez años.
 He lived in Madrid ten years.

70 Irregular verbs in the past historic

There is an important group of verbs that are irregular in the past historic (sometimes called the past definite). The endings are the same for all of them but the *stem* changes. Here are three examples (the stem changes are italicized):

andar (to walk)	**hacer** (to do/to make)	**venir** (to come)
and*uv*e	h*i*ce	v*i*ne
and*uv*iste	h*i*ciste	v*i*niste
and*uv*o	h*i*zo	v*i*no
and*uv*imos	h*i*cimos	v*i*nimos
and*uv*isteis	h*i*cisteis	v*i*nisteis
and*uv*ieron	h*i*cieron	v*i*nieron

Other verbs belonging to the same group are listed below, with their irregular stems:

estar (to be)	est*uv*-
decir (to say)	d*ij*-
saber (to know)	s*up*-
poner (to put)	p*us*-
poder (to be able)	p*ud*-
conducir (to drive)	cond*uj*-
querer (to want)	qu*is*-
haber (to have)	h*ub*-
tener (to have)	t*uv*-
traer (to bring)	tra*j*-

No quiso abrir la puerta.
 He didn't want to open the door.
Estuve enfermo dos meses.
 I was sick for two months.
No pudieron venir juntos.
 They weren't able to come together.

Note that the 3rd person plural of **decir, conducir, traer,** is **dijeron, condujeron, trajeron** (the "i" of the ending is omitted after the "j").

71 Past historic of "ser" and "ir"

Ser and ir have the same irregular forms in the past historic:

fui	fuimos
fuiste	fuisteis
fue	fueron

El verano pasado fui a Mallorca.
Last summer I went to Mallorca.
Fue un hombre muy famoso.
He was a very famous man.

72 Past historic of "dar" (to give)

di	dimos
diste	disteis
dio	dieron

Me dio un recado para Vd.
He gave me a message for you.
Les di tres mil pesetas.
I gave them three thousand pesetas.

73 Radical-changing verbs in the past historic

There is a small group of verbs ending in -ir that are irregular in the 3rd persons (singular and plural) of the past historic. The "e" in the stem becomes "i" and the "o" becomes "u." The rest of the tense is regular. Here are some examples:

	3rd pers. sing.	3rd pers. pl.
seguir (to follow)	siguió	siguieron
pedir (to ask for)	pidió	pidieron
sentir (to feel)	sintió	sintieron
dormir (to sleep)	durmió	durmieron
morir (to die)	murió	murieron

Durmió solamente cuatro horas.
He only slept four hours.
Pidieron dos botellas de vino.
They asked for two bottles of wine.

Vocabulary

dar un paseo	to go for a walk
por	along
el río	river
el sobre	envelope
pagar	to pay
la comida	meal
el cheque	check (in a restaurant)
el camarero	waiter
el kilómetro	kilometer
la hora de comer	lunchtime

Exercise 35

Translate:

1 We went for a walk along the river.
2 They didn't want to see me.
3 I put the letter in the envelope.
4 He died two years later.
5 He paid for the meal with a check.
6 The waiter brought us the drinks and went away.
7 They walked five kilometers looking for an auto-body shop.
8 I went out at ten o'clock and returned at lunchtime.
9 We told him that his father had arrived.
10 He didn't do anything all morning.

74 Imperfect and past historic contrasted

It is sometimes difficult for the student to decide whether to use the imperfect or the past historic, since, at times, they can both be translated by the English "did." Remember that the imperfect tells us what was going on, what somebody was doing or used to do over an indefinite period of time, whereas the past historic expresses what happened or what somebody did at a particular time. Study the following examples:

Nadábamos en el río todos los días.
 We swam (used to swim) in the river every day.
Ayer nadamos en el río.
 Yesterday we swam in the river.
Siempre fumaba un puro después de cenar.
 He always smoked (used to smoke) a cigar after dinner.
Anoche fumó un puro después de cenar.
 Last night he smoked a cigar after dinner.
Llovía cuando salimos del hotel.
 It was raining when we left the hotel.
Llovió toda la tarde.
 It rained all afternoon.

Vocabulary

la ducha	shower
sonar (ue)	to sound, to ring
jugar (ue)	to play
mientras	while
bajar	to go down
la cuenta	bill
hacer la maleta	to pack
cansado (-a)	tired
la (tarjeta) postal	postcard
el policía	police officer
preguntar	to ask

Exercise 36

Change the infinitives in parantheses to the correct form of the imperfect or past historic as appropriate.

1 Aquella mañana Ramón (salir) de su casa a las nueve.
2 Yo (estar) en la ducha cuando (sonar) el teléfono.
3 Cuando Carmen y María (viajar) a Valencia (tener) un accidente.
4 Los niños (jugar) en el jardín cuando (empezar) a llover.
5 Juan (bajar) a pagar la cuenta, mientras yo (hacer) la maleta.
6 Mi padre siempre (sentarse) en el mismo sillón.
7 Yo (volver) a casa muy cansada.
8 (Hacer) frío cuando nosotros (llegar) a Bilbao.
9 Luis (recibir) una postal de un amigo que (vivir) en Londres.
10 El policía me (preguntar) mi nombre y dirección.

75 The two verbs "to know"

It is important to differentiate between the verbs **saber** and **conocer**, both meaning "to know." **Saber** is to know a fact. **Conocer** is "to be acquainted with." For example:

No sabemos cuando llegará.
   We don't know when he will arrive.
Sé que está enfermo.
   I know that he is sick.
Conocemos a tu hermana muy bien.
   We know your sister very well.
No conozco* esa ciudad.
   I don't know that town.

*The verb **conocer** and a few others ending in -**cer** and -**cir** preceded by a vowel take a **z** before the **c** in the 1st person of the present indicative. The rest of the tense is regular.

conocer (to know)	→ conozco (I know)
obedecer (to obey)	→ obedezco (I obey)
pertenecer (to belong)	→ pertenezco (I belong)
conducir (to drive)	→ conduzco (I drive)
traducir (to translate)	→ traduzco (I translate)

76 Superlative of adjectives

The superlative is formed by putting **el más, la más, los más, las más,** in front of the adjective. For example:

Este hombre es el más pobre del pueblo.
This man is the poorest in the village.
Nuestra casa es la más grande de la calle.
Our house is the biggest in the street.

When the superlative immediately follows the noun, the article is omitted:

Es el edificio más alto de Madrid.
It is the highest building in Madrid.
Es la novela más interesante que he leído.
It is the most interesting novel I have read.

77 Superlative of adverbs

The superlative is formed by putting **lo más** in front of the adverb. (**Lo** is the neuter form of the definite article.)

Hágalo Vd. lo más pronto posible.
Do it as soon as possible.
Les escribiré el martes lo más tarde.
I'll write to them on Tuesday at the latest.

78 The absolute superlative of adjectives and adverbs

The ending **-ísimo** added to adjectives or adverbs translates the English "most," "extremely":

Es una mujer inteligentísima.
  She is an extremely intelligent woman.
Es un libro aburridísimo.
  It is an extremely boring book.
Llegaron al aeropuerto tardísimo.
  They arrived at the airport extremely late.
Hoy me he levantado tempranísimo.
  Today I have gotten up extremely early.

Vocabulary

el disco	record
el ordenador	computer
el programa de televisión	television program
divertido	amusing
la talla	size
amable	kind
interesante	interesting
la conversación	conversation
viejo	old
la farmacia	drugstore
la parada de autobús	bus stop

Exercise 37

Translate:

1 They don't know that record.
2 He knows that I want a computer.
3 That television program is most amusing.
4 This size is the smallest we have.
5 These shoes are the prettiest, those are the cheapest.
6 He is the kindest man I know.
7 They don't know that I want to see them.
8 It was a most interesting conversation.
9 It is the oldest church in this town.
10 The drugstore was extremely far from the bus stop.

79 The neuter article "lo"

We have already seen examples of **lo** preceding

a) an adverb:
Contestó lo mejor que pudo.
  He answered as best he could.

b) the relative **que**:
Lo que quiero decir.
  What I want to say.

Lo may also precede an adjective, thus making it an abstract noun:

Lo difícil es conseguir el dinero.
  The difficult thing is to obtain the money.
Lo importante es llegar a tiempo.
  The important thing is to arrive on time.

80 Uses of the definite and indefinite articles

The definite article is used in Spanish in the following cases:

a) before nouns used in a general sense:

El vino es barato en España.
Wine is cheap in Spain.

b) before abstract nouns:

El amor es ciego.
Love is blind.

c) before titles:

La reina Isabel de Inglaterra.
Queen Elizabeth of England.
El señor y la señora Ruiz/Los señores Ruiz.
Mr. and Mrs. Ruiz.

d) before names of institutions, public places, etc.:

el hospital (hospital), **la iglesia** (church), **la universidad** (university)

e) before proper nouns qualified by an adjective:

El pobre Carlos. Poor Charles.
El viejo Madrid. Old Madrid.

f) before parts of the body and articles of clothing, when in English the possessive adjective would be used:

Se ha roto la pierna.
He has broken his leg.
Me pondré el abrigo azul.
I will put on my blue coat.

g) before days of the week, seasons, and certain expressions of time:

Volveremos el martes. We will return on Tuesday.
El invierno se acerca. Winter is approaching.
Le vi la semana pasada. I saw him last week.

h) in certain set expressions:

El diez por ciento de rebaja. Ten percent reduction.
Sesenta pesetas el kilo. Sixty pesetas per kilo.

The indefinite article *is* used before an abstract noun qualified by an adjective, for example:

Condujo a una velocidad increíble.
   He drove at an incredible speed.

But it is *not* used:

a) before a noun indicating occupation, nationality, religion, or politics:

Es contable. He is an accountant.
Es española. She is Spanish.
Soy protestante. I am a Protestant.
¿Es Vd. conservador? Are you a conservative?

However, if the noun is qualified by an adjective, the article is used:

Es un buen contable.
   He is a good accountant.

b) before certain words: **otro** (another), **cierto** (certain), **medio** (half a), **cien** (a hundred), **mil** (a thousand), **tal** (such a), **¡qué!** (what a!)

Voy a comprar otro periódico.
   I am going to buy another newspaper.
Cierta mujer que conozco.
   A certain woman I know.

Medio litro de leche.
  Half a liter of milk.
¡Qué desastre!
  What a disaster!

Vocabulary

ponerse	to put on
el guante	glove
la dependienta	salesperson (f.)
principal	main
preocuparse	to worry
romper(se)	to break
derecho	right
el brazo	arm
hoy día	nowadays
la dificultad	difficulty
la botella	bottle
el coñac	brandy

Exercise 38

Translate:

1 Tea is a very nice drink.
2 Mrs. Collado will arrive on Sunday.
3 She put on her gloves because it was cold.
4 He is a waiter and she is a sales clerk.
5 I spent two weeks in the hospital.
6 The main thing is not to worry.
7 Poor Mary has broken her right arm.
8 Books are very expensive nowadays.
9 He used to walk with great difficulty.
10 He is going to bring another cup.
11 We drank half a bottle of brandy.
12 The best thing is to sell the house.

Drills

16 Yo no quería invitar a Carmen … pero tuve que
invitarla.
I didn't want to invite Carmen … but I had to
invite her.

Nosotros no queríamos ir a la playa … pero
tuvimos que ir.
We didn't want to go to the beach … but we had to go.

1 Pedro no quería escribir la carta …
2 Ellos no querían pagar la cuenta …
3 Yo no quería ver a Juan …
4 Nosotros no queríamos ir a la fiesta …
5 Vd. no quería salir del hotel …
6 Carmen no quería hacer la comida …
7 El niño no quería comer el pescado …
8 María no quería fumar un cigarrillo …
9 Yo no quería darle mi nombre …
10 Nosotros no queríamos beber la cerveza …

17 ¿Has hablado con Pedro hoy? Have you spoken with
Pedro today?
No, hablé ayer. No, I spoke yesterday.

¿Han visto Vds. a Conchita hoy? Have you seen Conchita
today?
No, la vimos ayer. No, we saw her yesterday.

1 ¿Han estado Vds. en la playa hoy?
2 ¿Han venido tus padres hoy?
3 ¿Ha comprado Vd. este libro hoy?
4 ¿Han pagado la cuenta hoy?
5 ¿Ha recibido Juan la postal hoy?
6 ¿Han hecho Vds. las maletas hoy?
7 ¿Ha llovido hoy?
8 ¿Han traído las flores hoy?
9 ¿Han ido Vds. al museo hoy?
10 ¿Ha visitado Vd. a sus amigos hoy?

18 Es una catedral muy grande. It's a very large cathedral.
Sí, es la más grande que he visto. Yes, it's the largest
I've seen.

1 Es un vestido muy bonito.
2 Son unos libros muy caros.
3 Es una playa muy grande.
4 Es un hotel muy elegante.
5 Son unos programas muy divertidos.
6 Son unas ventanas muy pequeñas.

CONVERSATION

Juan y Paloma hablan de lo que han hecho durante el fin de semana
Juan and Paloma talk about what they have done during the weekend

Juan El sábado me levanté muy tarde porque estaba cansadísimo de trabajar tanto durante la semana.
On Saturday I got up very late because I was exhausted after working so hard during the week.

Paloma ¿A qué le llamas tú tarde?
What do you call late?

Juan A las doce y media o la una. Era casi la hora de comer. Mi mujer no estaba muy contenta porque quería ir de compras conmigo por la mañana.
Twelve-thirty or one o'clock. It was almost lunchtime. My wife wasn't very pleased because she wanted to go shopping with me in the morning.

Paloma Así que tuviste que ir por la tarde.
So you had to go in the afternoon.

Juan Claro. Y fue larguísimo porque las tiendas estaban llenas de gente. Así que cuando volvimos, mi mujer preparó una cena rápida y nos sentamos a ver la televisión hasta las once y media.
Of course. And it was endless, because the stores were crowded. So, when we got back, my wife prepared a quick supper and we sat down to watch television until 11:30.

Paloma Yo fui a una boda el sábado. Se casaba un primo mío.
I went to a wedding on Saturday. A cousin of mine was getting married.

Juan   ¿Te divertiste?
         Did you have a good time?

Paloma Sí, estuvo muy bien. La comida fue buenísima,
         y la bebida también, claro. Hubo música y
         baile hasta las tres de la mañana.
         Yes, it was fine. The food was very good and the
         drinks too, of course. There was music and dancing
         till three in the morning.

Juan   Y el domingo ¿qué hiciste?
         And Sunday, what did you do?

Paloma Nada importante. Dormir, leer el periódico y
         ver la televisión ¿Y tú?
         Nothing important. Sleep, read the paper, and watch
         television. And you?

Juan   Poco más o menos, lo mismo que tú.
         More or less the same as you.

Chapter 10

The passive voice makes its first appearance. Learn how to form it and how to avoid using it.
Other subjects in Chapter 10 include:

- *the different uses of "**por**" and "**para**," both meaning "for"*
- *more spelling changes in verbs, to preserve the original pronunciation*
- *which verbs are followed directly by an infinitive, and which take a preposition before the infinitive*

81 "Por" and "para"

It is important to learn the uses of **por** and **para**, particularly since either word may translate the English "for."

Por is used to indicate means, motive, exchange. It translates the English: by, through, because of, out of, for the sake of, for:

Le di las gracias por las flores.
I thanked him for the flowers.
El ladrón entró por la ventana.
The thief came in through the window.
Lo hizo por nosotros.
He did it for us.
Envié el equipaje por tren.
I sent the luggage by train.

Para is used to indicate purpose, suitability, or destination. It translates the English: for, to, in order to, so as to:

Necesito dinero para comprar los billetes.
I need money to buy the tickets.
Este abrigo es demasiado grande para mí.
This coat is too big for me.
El tren sale para Málaga dentro de cinco minutos.
The train leaves for Malaga within five minutes.
Es un regalo para Vd.
It is a present for you.

There are also many idiomatic uses of **por** and **para** that you will learn by observation. Here are some examples:

Estamos para salir. We are about to go out.
Estoy por no hacerlo. I am inclined not to do it.
Lo dejaremos para mañana. We will leave it for tomorrow.
Una vez por semana. Once a week.
Por la tarde. In the afternoon (evening).
Por ejemplo. For example.
Por último. Finally.
Por consiguiente. Therefore, consequently.
Por lo visto. Evidently.

Vocabulary

joven	young
el sacrificio	sacrifice
pasar	to pass
la Aduana	customs
cobrar	to charge
el cine	movies
las compras	purchases, shopping
la llave	key
el armario	cupboard, wardrobe
difícil	difficult
el avión	airplane
cualquier cosa	anything
la curiosidad	curiosity
el melocotón	peach

Exercise 39

Fill in the gaps with "por" or "para" as appropriate:

1 Pagó cien mil pesetas _____ el coche.
2 No podemos salir _____ esa puerta.
3 Voy de vacaciones _____ descansar.
4 Le llamaré _____ teléfono mañana.
5 Estas cartas no son _____ mí.
6 Es demasiado joven _____ comprenderlo.
7 Hizo ese sacrificio _____ su padre.
8 Hay que tener mucho dinero _____ viajar.
9 Saldremos _____ Valencia el martes.
10 No pudo venir a la fiesta _____ estar enfermo.

Exercise 40

Translate:

1 We have to pass through customs.
2 They charged us two thousand pesetas for the meal.
3 It is too late to go to the movies.
4 I need a bag for all my shopping.
5 Have you (*pol.*) a key to open this cupboard?
6 This book is too difficult for him.
7 The plane leaves for Madrid at a quarter after seven.
8 I would do anything for him.
9 We read the letter out of curiosity.
10 She wants to buy some peaches for her mother.

82 The passive voice

The passive voice is formed with the verb **ser** followed by
the past participle. The agent is usually introduced by **por**,
although **de** is sometimes used after verbs of feeling and in
some set expressions such as **cubierto de** (covered by),
acompañado de (accompanied by). In the passive voice the
past participle agrees in gender and number with the subject.

La carta fue firmada por el presidente.
The letter was signed by the president.
El soldado fue herido por una bala.
The soldier was wounded by a bullet.

Note that the past participle is also used with **estar** to indicate state, whereas with **ser** it indicates action. Compare the following examples:

El libro está publicado en cinco idiomas.
The book is published in five languages.
El libro será publicado en cinco idiomas.
The book will be published in five languages.

83 Avoidance of the passive voice

The passive voice is less frequently used in Spanish than in English, and it is often avoided by one of the following means:

a) by using the reflexive pronoun **se**:

Se prohibe fumar. Smoking is forbidden.
El museo se cierra a las seis. The museum is closed at six.

Se also translates the English "one":

No se puede decir. One cannot tell.

b) by using the 3rd person plural of the verb as an impersonal form:

Nos vieron salir de la casa.
They saw us (we were seen) leaving the house.
Dicen que no va a volver.
They say (it is said) that he is not coming back.

c) by changing the roles of subject and agent, using the active voice:

Le paró la policía. He was stopped by the police.

Vocabulary

construir	to build
el abuelo	grandfather
acusar	to accuse
el robo	theft
el barco	boat
ahora	now
creer	to believe
muerto	dead
la montaña	mountain
cubierto	covered
la nieve	snow
la cena	dinner
servir (i)	to serve
pintar	to paint
recibir	to receive
el director	director
presentar	to introduce
famoso	famous
el actor	actor

Exercise 41

Translate:

1 The house was built by his grandfather.
2 I was accused of the theft.
3 The boat was sold for eighty thousand pesetas.
4 The work is now finished.
5 It is believed that he is dead.
6 The mountains were covered in snow.
7 Dinner is not served until nine.
8 The windows were painted three weeks ago.
9 They were received by one of the directors.
10 The program was introduced by a famous actor.

84 Changes of spelling in verbs

Certain verbs have a change of spelling in the stem, in some parts of the conjugation, in order to preserve the original pronunciation. Verbs ending in:

-car change the **c** into **qu** before e:
buscar (to look for) → **busqué** (I looked for)

-zar change the **z** into **c** before e:
empezar (to begin) → **empecé** (I began)

-gar change the **g** into **gu** before e:
pagar (to pay) → **pagué** (I paid)

-ger or **-gir** change the **g** into **j** before a or o:
coger (to pick up)   → **cojo** (I pick up)
dirigir (to direct)   → **dirija Vd.** (direct)

Note that an unaccented **i** between two vowels is always changed to **y**:

leer (to read)	→ **leyó, leyeron** (he/they read)
creer (to think)	→ **creyó, creyeron** (he/they thought)
huir (to flee)	→ **huyó, huyeron** (he/they fled)
construir (to build)	→ **construyó, construyeron** (he/they built)
oír (to hear)	→ **oyó, oyeron** (he/they heard)
caer (to fall)	→ **cayó, cayeron** (he/they fell)

These changes also occur in the present participle:

leyendo (reading), **creyendo** (thinking), **huyendo** (fleeing), **construyendo** (building), **oyendo** (hearing), **cayendo** (falling)

Vocabulary

el aparcamiento	parking lot
el ruido	noise
arriba	upstairs, above
secar(se)	to dry (oneself)
el pie	foot
al fuego	by the fire
el suelo	ground, floor
las instrucciones	instructions
el principio	beginning
la guerra	war
el cuadro	picture
el equipaje	luggage

Exercise 42

Translate:

1 I played with the children all afternoon.
2 They are building a new parking lot.
3 He heard a noise upstairs.
4 I dried my feet by the fire.
5 They fell to the ground.
6 He is reading the instructions.
7 They fled from Spain at the beginning of the war.
8 I paid a lot of money for that picture.
9 Pick up the luggage, please.
10 He thought that the store was closed.

85 Verbs followed by an infinitive

Some Spanish verbs may be directly followed by an infinitive, while others take a preposition before the infinitive. The following lists include some of the most common verbs belonging to either of these categories.

- Verbs directly followed by an infinitive:

  aconsejar (to advise)
  Me aconsejó esperar.
    He advised me to wait.

  conseguir (to manage to)
  Conseguimos abrirlo.
    We managed to open it.

  deber (must)
  Debo visitarla más a menudo.
    I must visit her more often.

  decidir (to decide)
  Decidió venir conmigo.
    He decided to come with me.

  esperar (to hope to)
  Esperamos verle en España.
    We hope to see him in Spain.

  intentar (to try to)
  Intenté encontrar un empleo.
    I tried to find a job.

  parecer (to appear to, to seem)
  Pareció ser una falsa alarma.
    It appeared to be a false alarm.

  pedir (to ask to)
  Ha pedido hablar con el gerente.
    He has asked to speak to the manager.

pensar (to intend)
Pienso salir muy temprano.
   I intend to leave very early.

poder (to be able to, can)
No podíamos ver nada.
   We could not see anything.

- Verbs followed by **a** + infinitive:

entrar (to come in)
Entró a preguntar el precio.
   He came in to ask the price.

empezar (to begin)
Empezó a comer.
   He began to eat.

enseñar (to teach)
Me enseñó a conducir.
   He taught me to drive.

aprender (to learn)
Aprendieron a nadar en seguida.
   They quickly learned to swim.

decidirse (to decide)
Me decidí a decírselo.
   I decided to tell him.

volver (to return)
Volvió a recoger su maleta.
   He came back to collect his suitcase.

Note that **volver a** can be used idiomatically with the meaning of "to do something again":

Volví a verle al día siguiente.
   I saw him again the following day.

- Verbs followed by **de** + infinitive:

  acabar (to finish)
  Acabó de leer la carta.
    He finished reading the letter.

  acabar de used in the present or imperfect indicative has the meaning of "to have just":

  Acabo de ver a Juan. I have just seen John.
  Acababan de salir. They had just gone out.

  acordarse (to remember)
  No se acordó de llevar su pasaporte.
    He didn't remember to take his passport.

  cansarse (to get tired)
  Me cansé de andar.
    I got tired of walking.

  dejar (to stop)
  El niño dejó de llorar.
    The child stopped crying.

  olvidarse (to forget)
  Se olvidaron de comprar gasolina.
    They forgot to buy gas.

  tratar (to try)
  Traté de verle.
    I tried to see him.

- Verbs followed by **en** + infinitive:

  consentir (to consent)
  Ha consentido en hablar con ella.
    He has consented to speak to her.

  insistir (to insist)
  Insistió en acompañarme.
    He insisted on accompanying me.

pensar (to think)
Pensaba en escribir a su amigo.
He was thinking of writing to his friend.

vacilar (to hesitate)
Vacilé en darle la noticia.
I hesitated to tell him the news.

tardar (to take time)
Tardó mucho en llegar.
He took a long time to arrive.

- Verbs followed by **por** + infinitive:

acabar (to finish)
Acabé por darle el dinero.
I finished by giving him the money.

empezar (to begin)
Empezaremos por aprender el alfabeto.
We will begin by learning the alphabet.

esforzarse (to make an effort)
Se esforzó por ser amable.
He made an effort to be kind.

- Verbs followed by **con** + infinitive:

amenazar (to threaten)
El hombre amenazó con disparar.
The man threatened to shoot.

soñar (to dream)
Sueña con hacer mucho dinero.
He dreams of making a lot of money.

contentarse (to content oneself)
Me contento con descansar unos minutos.
I content myself with resting for a few minutes.

Vocabulary

alquilar	to hire, to rent
quejarse de	to complain
el servicio	service
jugar a	to play (a game)
el tenis	tennis
telefonear	to phone, to call up
subir	to climb
el paquete	parcel
la discusión	argument
sonreir (i)	to smile
ganar	to earn

Exercise 43

Translate:

1 I managed to speak with them.
2 He advised us to rent a car.
3 They tried to come into the room.
4 I intend to complain about the service.
5 We are learning to play tennis.
6 I called him up again.
7 Mr. Solís has just arrived.
8 He got tired of climbing and sat down.
9 It stopped raining and the sun came out.
10 I forgot to give him the message.
11 They insisted on paying for their tickets.
12 The package took two weeks to arrive.
13 They finished by having an argument.
14 The woman made an effort to smile.
15 The man threatened to call the police.
16 He is content with earning very little.

Drills

19 *Fill in the blanks with either "por" or "para" as appropriate:*

1 ¿Necesitas dinero?
Sí, _____ comprar los sellos.
2 ¿Ha comprado el vestido?
Sí, _____ cuatro mil pesetas.
3 ¿Lleva Vd. un libro?
Sí, _____ leer en la playa.
4 ¿Has comprado un regalo?
Sí, _____ mi madre.
5 ¿Ha enviado Vd. el paquete?
Sí, _____ avión.
6 ¿Salen Vds. mañana?
Sí, _____ América.
7 ¿Necesitas gafas?
Sí, _____ leer solamente.
8 ¿Han dado Vds. un paseo?
Sí, _____ el borde del río.

20 *Avoid the passive voice by using the reflexive pronoun "se," as in the following example:*

El piso fue vendido. The apartment was sold.
El piso se vendió. The apartment was sold.

1 El libro fue publicado.
2 Los coches fueron alquilados.
3 La puerta fue abierta.
4 Los ruidos fueron oídos.
5 El trabajo fue terminado.
6 La casa fue construida.
7 Los barcos fueron vendidos.
8 La carta fue leída.

21 ¿Has visto a mi hermano? Have you seen my brother?
Sí, acabo de verle. Yes, I have just seen him.

1 ¿Ha comprado Vd. los zapatos?
2 ¿Han llegado los invitados?
3 ¿Ha recibido Vd. las cartas?
4 ¿Han hecho Vds. las compras?
5 ¿Se han acostado los niños?
6 ¿Ha encontrado Vd. la llave?

CONVERSATION

Marisa y Manolo se encuentran en una cafetería
Marisa and Manolo meet in a Spanish cafeteria

Manolo ¡Por fin! Creí que no venías. Llevo aquí más de media hora.
At last! I thought you weren't coming. I have been here more than half an hour.

Marisa Lo siento, Manolo. Mi padre necesitaba el coche para ir a ver a unos clientes y he tenido que venir en autobús.
I'm sorry, Manolo. My father needed the car to go and see some clients and I had to come by bus.

Manolo Pero el autobús suele ser rápido.
But the bus is usually quick.

Marisa Generalmente, sí. Pero hoy hemos encontrado una manifestación en la Plaza de San Pedro y el autobús no podía pasar.
Usually it is. But today we ran into a demonstration in St. Peter's Square and the bus could not get through.

Manolo Y ¿para qué era la manifestación?
And what was the demonstration for?

Marisa No sé. No he conseguido enterarme. Pero había muchos jóvenes que no dejaban de gritar y que insistían en ponerse delante del autobús.
I don't know. I didn't manage to find out. But there were many youngsters who would not stop shouting and who insisted on standing in front of the bus.

Manolo ¡Siempre hay algún jaleo! Bueno ¿qué vas a tomar?
There is always some trouble! Well, what are you going to have?

Marisa **Tengo sed. Creo que empezaré por tomar una cerveza y después, quizás, algo de comer.**
I'm thirsty. I think that I'll start by having a beer and then, perhaps, something to eat.

Manolo **Yo acababa de tomar una ginebra con tónica cuando has llegado. Pero voy a tomar otra y un bocadillo de jamón porque tengo hambre.**
I had just had a gin and tonic when you arrived. But I am going to have another one and a ham sandwich, because I'm hungry.

Marisa **¿Qué vamos a hacer después?**
What are we going to do later?

Manolo **Pues había pensado ir al cine ¿que te parece?**
Well, I thought we could go to the movies. What do you think?

Marisa **Sí, buena idea. Hay varias películas que me gustaría ver.**
Yes, good idea. There are several movies that I would like to see.

Manolo **Ahora decidiremos. Primero voy a llamar al camarero.**
We'll decide now. First I am going to call the waiter.

Revision – 3

Exercise 1

Put the underlined verbs in the following sentences into the future tense:

1 <u>Vamos</u> de paseo después de comer.
2 Pilar <u>cuida</u> a los niños.
3 <u>Trabajo</u> dos días por semana.
4 <u>Se levanta</u> a las ocho.
5 <u>Salimos</u> a cenar con unos amigos.
6 <u>Viene</u> a vernos el domingo.
7 <u>Hace</u> buen tiempo todo el verano.
8 Se lo <u>dio</u> al camarero.
9 Este año no <u>pueden</u> ir de vacaciones.
10 Ahora <u>tienes</u> que hablar español.

Exercise 2

This deals with reported speech. Study the examples to see what you have to do, then complete the exercise:

Hablaré al gerente.	I'll speak to the manager.
Dijo que hablaría al gerente.	He said he would speak to the manager.
Hablaremos al gerente.	We'll speak to the manager.
Dijeron que hablarían al gerente.	They said they would speak to the manager.

1 Traeré las maletas. Dijo que ____
2 Volveremos a las cinco. Dijeron que ____
3 Viajaré en avión. Dijo que ____
4 Pagaremos por cheque. Dijeron que ____
5 Enviaré una postal. Dijo que ____
6 Tendrán que saberlo pronto. Dijeron que ____

Exercise 3

Translate:

1 Last night I saw Antonio with his wife.
2 The train arrived two hours late.
3 He offered to help me with the bags.
4 We didn't need any winter clothes.
5 They sold the house to a friend of theirs.
6 I drove 100 kms. without stopping.
7 He went to look for a drugstore.
8 She didn't like the book I gave her.

Exercise 4

Back in the United States after a short holiday in Spain with your wife, you meet a Spanish friend, Alberto, who asks you what you did. Translate what he says, then answer by translating the English lines.

Alberto	¿Qué tal lo pasasteis en España?
Usted	Very well. It was a very interesting journey.
Alberto	¿Adónde fuisteis?
Usted	We went to Córdoba, Granada, and Sevilla.
Alberto	¡Qué bien! ¿Habíais estado antes en esas ciudades?
Usted	My wife had been to Sevilla, but I didn't know any of them.
Alberto	¿Cuál de ellas te gustó más?
Usted	I don't know. It's difficult to choose one. Each one has a different beauty. Possibly Granada. The Alhambra is wonderful.
Alberto	Sí, a mí también me gusta mucho Granada, pero de las tres prefiero Sevilla. Sevilla tiene un encanto especial para mí.
Usted	Alberto, I would like to go on talking, but I have to go shopping with my wife. She'll be waiting for me. I'll call you on Friday.
Alberto	Sí, a ver si tomamos una copa juntos. Adiós.

Exercise 5

Translate:

1 Why do you need the money?
2 I need it to buy a new car.
3 They left yesterday for Venezuela.
4 I am doing this for you (for your sake).
5 We are too tired to walk to the station.
6 The hotel costs eight thousand pesetas per person.
7 He invited me to his house for a month.
8 They sent me a card to tell me they were coming.

Exercise 6

These sentences are all in the passive voice. Rewrite them using one of the means of avoidance given in section 83:

1 Los vuelos han sido cancelados.
2 Fue acompañado por su mujer.
3 La película ha sido censurada.
4 Las elecciones fueron anunciadas en octubre.
5 El muchacho fue arrestado por la policía.
6 La exposición fue inaugurada por el Rey.
7 La explosión fue oída en todo el pueblo.
8 El cheque no ha sido aceptado por el banco.

Exercise 7

Put the correct prepositions after the verbs in the following sentences, if appropriate:

1 Se cansó _____ estudiar y salió _____ dar un paseo.
2 Mi padre me enseñó_____ nadar.
3 Intentamos _____ comprar billetes, pero estaba todo vendido.
4 Me ha prometido que va _____ dejar _____ fumar.
5 La carta tardó _____ llegar cinco días.
6 Al salir del cine empezó _____ llover.
7 Volví _____ telefonear, pero no contestaron.   →

8 Consiguió _____ encontrar un empleo en una fábrica.
9 Como no venía el autobús, decidimos _____ tomar
   un taxi.
10 Acabo _____ leer una novela buenísima.
11 Insistieron _____ devolverme el dinero.
12 Espero _____ recibir el paquete mañana.
13 María está aprendiendo_____ conducir.
14 Pensamos _____ viajar por toda España.
15 Se olvidaron _____ darnos su dirección.
16 Siempre sueña _____ volver a su país.

Exercise 8

Translate:
1 We are all tired today.
2 My son wants to be a lawyer.
3 When he was sick, I used to visit him every day.
4 Don't sit (*fam.sing.*) in that chair, it's broken.
5 It's very hot, although all the windows are open.
6 He is sad because his best friend has died.
7 I am always at home on Sundays.
8 She is a very intelligent woman, but not very kind.
9 Who are you (*pol. sing.*)? I am a friend of hers.
10 We were about to leave when he arrived.
11 They didn't give him the job because he was too young.
12 These are not my suitcases, mine are black.

Exercise 9

*Put the verbs in brackets into the correct form of the imperfect
tense or the past historic, as appropriate:*

1 Siempre que nosotros [ir] a Italia [quedarse] en el
   mismo hotel.
2 El policía me [hacer] parar el coche y me [pedir] el
   pasaporte.
3 Les dije que no [tener] dinero y no [poder] pagar la
   multa.

4 Carmen le [llamar] a la oficina, pero él no [estar].

5 Nosotros [llevar] media hora esperando cuando [llegar] el tren.

6 Ellos [ir] a ver Toledo, pero [volver] pronto porque [hacer] mucho frío.

7 Cuando yo [llegar] al restaurante, mi hermana ya [estar] allí.

8 El portero me [dejar] entrar cuando le [dar] una propina.

9 El avión [salir] con mucho retraso porque [haber] niebla.

10 Pedro [trabajar] durante diez años en una oficina que [estar] cerca de mi casa.

Chapter 11

The subjunctive mood, its uses, and the formation of its present and perfect tenses, take up much of this chapter. Other topics include:

- *uses of the verb "**deber**" to mean "must," "should," and "ought" as well as "to owe"*
- *the familiar imperative*
- *idiomatic uses of "**seguir**" and "**valer**"*

86 Uses of the verb "deber"

Deber followed by an infinitive translates the English "must":

Debemos salir temprano.
  We must leave early.
No debes fumar tanto.
  You must not smoke so much.

Used in the conditional, **deber** translates "should" and "ought":

Vd. no debería hablar así.
  You should not speak like that.
Deberíamos tener más cuidado.
  We ought to be more careful.

Deber de followed by an infinitive translates "must" (expressing assumption):

Deben de tener mucha hambre.
They must be very hungry.
El avión debe de haber llegado ya.
The plane must have arrived already.

Deber also means "to owe":

Deben mucho dinero. They owe a lot of money.

87 "Saber" and "poder"

It is important not to confuse these two verbs when translating the English "can." Compare the following examples:

¿Sabe Vd. conducir?
Can you drive? (= Do you know how to?)

¿Puede Vd. conducir?
Can you drive? (= Are you physically able to?)

Vocabulary

la cosa	thing
las gafas	glasses
allí	there
a menudo	often
la explicación	explanation
la sortija	ring
costar (ue)	to cost
montar en bicicleta	to ride a bicycle
la píldora	pill
guisar	to cook

Exercise 44

Translate:

1 How much do I owe you (*pol.*)?
2 They should not say those things.
3 She must have a good job.
4 I must see a doctor.
5 Can he speak Spanish?
6 I cannot read without glasses.
7 We should go there more often.
8 He owes me an explanation.
9 That ring must cost a lot of money.
10 I cannot ride a bicycle.
11 He cannot sleep without taking pills.
12 Can you (*pol.*) cook?

88 The present subjunctive

a) Regular verbs
The present subjunctive tense of regular verbs is conjugated thus:

hablar	comer	vivir
hable	coma	viva
hables	comas	vivas
hable	coma	viva
hablemos	comamos	vivamos
habléis	comáis	viváis
hablen	coman	vivan

b) Radical-changing verbs
Radical-changing verbs of the first and second conjugations have the same stem changes as in the present indicative:

cerrar (ie)	volver (ue)
cierre	vuelva
cierres	vuelvas
cierre	vuelva
cerremos	volvamos
cerréis	volváis
cierren	vuelvan

Radical-changing verbs of the third conjugation have a stem change *also* in the 1st and 2nd persons plural, **e** changes to **i** and **o** changes to **u**:

pedir (i)	sentir (ie)	dormir (ue)
pida	sienta	duerma
pidas	sientas	duermas
pida	sienta	duerma
pidamos	sintamos	durmamos
pidáis	sintáis	durmáis
pidan	sientan	duerman

c) Other irregular verbs

The stem of the present subjunctive of most irregular verbs is the same as that of the 1st person singular of the present indicative. For instance:

	Present indic.	*Present subjunctive*
tener	tengo	tenga, -as, -a, etc.
venir	vengo	venga, -as, -a, etc.
traer	traigo	traiga, -as, -a, etc.
conocer	conozco	conozca, -as, -a, etc.

The exceptions to this rule are: **dar, estar, haber, ir, saber,** and **ser:**

dar	estar	haber
dé	esté	haya
des	estés	hayas
dé	esté	haya
demos	estemos	hayamos
deis	estéis	hayáis
den	estén	hayan

ir	saber	ser
vaya	sepa	sea
vayas	sepas	seas
vaya	sepa	sea
vayamos	sepamos	seamos
vayáis	sepáis	seáis
vayan	sepan	sean

As the 1st and 3rd persons singular of the present subjunctive have the same endings, the subject pronoun is sometimes used to avoid ambiguity.

89 The perfect subjunctive

The perfect subjunctive is formed with the present subjunctive of **haber** followed by the appropriate past participle:

... que hayan salido ...
 ... that they may have gone out ...
... que hayamos visto ...
 ... that we may have seen ...

90 Uses of the subjunctive

The subjunctive is generally used in dependent clauses in which the action of the verb is presented not as a reality, but as a possibility, something that is yet to happen. It is used:

a) after verbs expressing wish, command, request, need, permission, prohibition, preference, doubt, emotion.
For example:

Quieren que cantemos. They want us to sing.
Necesito que me ayudes. I need you to help me.

Prefiero que Vd. lo haga. I prefer you to do it.
Me prohiben que vaya. They forbid me to go.
Siento que esté Vd. enfermo. I am sorry you are sick.

Note that when the subject of the dependent verb is the same as that of the main verb, the infinitive construction is used:

Quieren cantar. They want to sing.
Prefiero hacerlo. I prefer to do it.

b) after impersonal expressions that indicate doubt, preference, possibility, probability, necessity:

Es preferible que esperemos. It's preferable that we wait.
Es dudoso que vengan. It's doubtful that they will come.
Es posible que lo sepa. It's possible that he knows it.

c) after certain conjunctions when they introduce an un-certain or future action:

Se lo daré cuando le vea.
    I'll give it to him when I see him.
Tendrán que pagarlo aunque no quieran.
    They'll have to pay for it even if they don't want to.

d) after the following related phrases:

antes de que	before
hasta que	until
para que	so as to
sin que	without
con tal que	provided that
a no ser que	unless
después de que	after

Lo terminaré antes de que llegue.
    I'll finish it before he arrives.
Saldremos sin que nos vean.
    We'll go out without their seeing us.

e) after relative pronouns with indefinite negative or interrogative antecedents:

¿Hay alguien que sepa donde está?
Is there anyone who knows where it is?
No hay un hombre que no quiera triunfar.
There is not a man who doesn't want to succeed.

f) after the following expressions when they introduce a future action:

quienquiera, quienesquiera	whoever
cualquiera, cualesquiera	whatever
comoquiera	however
cuandoquiera	whenever
dondequiera	wherever

No quiero verle, quienquiera que sea.
I don't want to see him, whoever he is.
Dondequiera que vaya, siempre llevo mi pasaporte.
Wherever I go, I always carry my passport.

"However" followed by an adjective or an adverb is always translated in Spanish by **por** + adjective/adverb + the subjunctive tense:

Por mucho que le quieras.
However much you love him.
Por caros que sean.
However expensive they may be.
Por estúpido que parezca.
However stupid it may seem.

Vocabulary

alegrarse	to be glad
el abogado	lawyer
el documento	document
mandar	to order
dudar	to doubt
sorprender	to surprise
perderse	to lose one's way
la lástima	pity
dejar	to let, to allow
el precio	price
tocar	to play (an instrument)
el piano	piano
cuidar de	to look after
el problema	problem
tener éxito	to succeed
la práctica	practice

Exercise 45

Translate:

1 I am glad they are able to come.
2 He wants the lawyer to see the documents.
3 They have ordered us to wait here.
4 I doubt that the sun will come out.
5 It surprises me that she has not written.
6 He has asked me to teach him Spanish.
7 It's possible that they have lost their way.
8 It's a pity that we don't have enough money.
9 It's probable that they will get married.
10 I won't be able to do it unless they help me.
11 We'll go to the movies, provided you let me pay.
12 He will wait until I return.
13 They will have to eat it, even if they don't like it.
14 There is no one who can pay that price.
15 Is there anyone who can play the piano?   →

16 I need a woman to look after the children.
17 We'll find it, wherever it is.
18 He will help you (*fam.sing.*), whenever you have
   a problem.
19 However much he may try, he will never succeed.
20 However easy it may seem, one needs practice.

91 The familiar imperative

The familiar imperative corresponds to the pronouns **tú** and
vosotros, whereas the polite imperative, as we have already
seen, corresponds to **Vd.** and **Vds.**

a) Regular verbs:

hablar	habla (tú)	hablad (vosotros)	speak!
comer	come (tú)	comed (vosotros)	eat!
vivir	vive (tú)	vivid (vosotros)	live!

b) Radical-changing verbs. Only the singular form is
irregular:

cerrar	cierra (tú)	cerrad (vosotros)	close!
volver	vuelve (tú)	volved (vosotros)	come back!
pedir	pide (tú)	pedid (vosotros)	ask!

c) Irregular verbs. Only the singular form is irregular:

decir	di (tú)	decid (vosotros)	say!
hacer	haz (tú)	haced (vosotros)	do!
ir	ve (tú)	id (vosotros)	go!
oír	oye (tú)	oíd (vosotros)	hear!
poner	pon (tú)	poned (vosotros)	put!
salir	sal (tú)	salid (vosotros)	go out!
ser	sé (tú)	sed (vosotros)	be!
tener	ten (tú)	tened (vosotros)	have!
venir	ven (tú)	venid (vosotros)	come!

The familiar imperative only exists in the positive form. In the negative form the 2nd persons singular and plural of the present subjunctive are used.

No hables (*s.*).	**no habléis** (*pl.*).	Don't speak.
No cierres (*s.*).	**no cerréis** (*pl.*).	Don't close.
No vayas (*s.*).	**no vayáis** (*pl.*).	Don't go.

Object and reflexive pronouns are attached to the end of the verb in the positive form, but they precede the verb in the negative form.

Míralo (*s.*).	**miradlo** (*pl.*).	Look at it.
No lo mires (*s.*).	**no lo miréis** (*pl.*).	Don't look at it.
Siéntate (*s.*).	**sentaos** (*pl.*).	Sit down.
No te sientes (*s.*).	**no os sentéis** (*pl.*).	Don't sit down.

Note that the final **d** of the plural form is omitted when the reflexive pronoun is attached. The exception is **"idos"** from the verb **ir**. Note also that in some cases an accent is used to preserve the original stress.

Exercise 46

Put the following verbs into the familiar imperative in both positive and negative forms, singular and plural:

1 Hacerlo.
2 Venir.
3 Acostarse.
4 Aprender.
5 Ponerlo.
6 Escribirla.
7 Gritar.
8 Oírlo.
9 Preocuparse.
10 Dormirse.

Vocabulary

enfadarse	to get angry
escuchar	to listen
vestirse (i)	to get dressed
callarse	to be quiet
despertar (ie)	to waken
perdonar	to forgive
el error	error
mover (ue)	to move

Exercise 47

Translate:

1 Don't get angry. (*s.*)
2 Listen to me. (*pl.*)
3 Get dressed. (*s.*)
4 Don't tell me that. (*pl.*)
5 Be careful. (*pl.*)
6 Read it to us. (*s.*)
7 Be quiet. (*pl.*)
8 Don't wake me up early. (*s.*)
9 Forgive my error. (*pl.*)
10 Don't move the car. (*s.*)

92 Idiomatic use of "seguir"

This verb has two meanings: "to follow" and, with the present participle of another verb, "to go on doing something":

El perro siguió a su amo.
　The dog followed his master.
Siga Vd. trabajando.
　Go on working.

"To go on doing something" can also be rendered by the verb **continuar** followed by the present participle:

La mujer continuó hablando.
  The woman went on talking.

93 Idiomatic use of "valer"

This verb can be translated by "to cost" or "to be worth":
¿Cuánto vale el billete?
  How much does the ticket cost?
Esta pulsera no vale nada.
  This bracelet is worthless.
No vale la pena.
  It isn't worth it.

Valer has the same irregularities in its conjugation as **salir**.

Drills

22 ¿Tiene mucho dinero? Does he have a lot of money?
Sí, debe de tener mucho dinero. Yes, he must have a lot
of money.

1 ¿Está enfermo?
2 ¿Son las cinco?
3 ¿Están muy tristes?
4 ¿Trabaja mucho?
5 ¿Hace muchos años?
6 ¿Están en casa?

23 ¿Vamos a esperar? Are we going to wait?
Sí, es preferible que esperemos. Yes, it's better if we wait.

1 ¿Van a comer?
2 ¿Va a irse?
3 ¿Vamos a volver?
4 ¿Van a acostarse?
5 ¿Va a pagar?
6 ¿Vamos a sentarnos?

24 ¿Cierro la puerta? Should I shut the door?
Sí, ciérrala. Yes, shut it.

1 ¿Pedimos los cafés?
2 ¿Traigo el vino?
3 ¿Llamamos a Miguel?
4 ¿Compro el regalo?
5 ¿Abrimos las ventanas?
6 ¿Ayudo a Pedro?

25 ¿Han terminado de hablar? Have they finished talking?
No, siguen hablando. No, they are still talking.

1 ¿Han terminado de comer?
2 ¿Ha terminado Juan de leer el periódico?
3 ¿Han terminado Vds. de trabajar?
4 ¿Ha terminado Vd. de pintar?
5 ¿Ha terminado Conchita de cantar?
6 ¿Han terminado de construir la casa?

CONVERSATION

La Sra. Ramos habla con su hijo Pablo, de quince años
Mrs. Ramos talks with her fifteen-year-old son, Pablo

Sra. Ramos Pablo, levántate que ya son las diez y media.
Pablo, get up. It's 10:30.

Pablo Déjame dormir un poco más. Es sábado y no tengo que ir al colegio.
Let me sleep a little longer. It's Saturday and I don't have to go to school.

Sra. Ramos No, pero necesito que vayas a hacerme unas compras.
No, but I need you to go and do some shopping for me.

Pablo ¿Por qué?
Why?

Sra. Ramos Porque yo no tengo tiempo de salir. Vienen unos invitados a cenar esta noche y tengo mucho que hacer en casa.
Because I don't have the time to go out. I have guests coming to dinner this evening and I have a lot to do in the house.

Pablo Y ¿adónde tengo que ir?
And where do I have to go?

Sra. Ramos Quiero que me traigas unas cosas del supermercado, ahora te haré una lista, y que recojas la carne de la carnicería.
I want you to bring me a few things from the supermarket – I'll make you a list now – and to pick up the meat from the butcher's.

Pablo	**Espero que no me lleve mucho tiempo hacer todo eso.**
	I hope it doesn't take me long to do all that.
Sra. Ramos	**Pues, cuanto antes te levantes, antes te pondrás en camino.**
	Well, the sooner you get up the sooner you'll be on your way.
Pablo	**¡Y yo que quería jugar al fútbol con mis amigos esta mañana!**
	And I wanted to play soccer with my friends this morning!
Sra. Ramos	**¡Vamos! Date prisa y tendrás tiempo para todo. Ya te he puesto el desayuno en la mesa.**
	Come on! Hurry up and you will have time for everything. I have already put your breakfast on the table.

Chapter 12

We continue to learn about the subjunctive: its imperfect
and pluperfect tenses, their formation and uses;
the sequence of tenses; when to use it in main clauses.
Also:

- "may" and "might"
- verbs followed by prepositions
- "al" followed by the infinitive

94 The imperfect subjunctive

The imperfect subjunctive has two forms, with different
endings. The stem is obtained by removing the ending
-ron from the 3rd person plural of the past historic: habla-,
comie-, vivie-, etc. To this stem the following endings are
added: -ra, -ras, -ra, -ramos, -rais, -ran or -se, -ses, -se,
semos, -seis, -sen.
Both forms are equally acceptable. It is very much a matter
of choice whether one or the other is used.

a) Regular verbs:

hablar	hablara, hablaras, etc.
	hablase, hablases, etc.
comer	comiera, comieras, etc.
	comiese, comieses, etc.
vivir	viviera, vivieras, etc.
	viviese, vivieses, etc.

b) Radical-changing verbs:

cerrar	cerrara, cerraras, etc.
	cerrase, cerrases, etc.
volver	volviera, volvieras, etc.
	volviese, volvieses, etc.
pedir	pidiera, pidieras, etc.
	pidiese, pidieses, etc.

c) Irregular verbs:

estar	estuviera, estuvieras, etc.
	estuviese, estuvieses, etc.
tener	tuviera, tuvieras, etc.
	tuviese, tuvieses, etc.
decir	dijera, dijeras, etc.
	dijese, dijeses, etc.

95 Pluperfect subjunctive

This tense is formed with the imperfect subjunctive of **haber** followed by the past participle of the appropriate verb:

Hubiera (hubiese) visto. He might have seen.
Hubiéramos (hubiésemos) vendido. We might have sold.

96 Uses of the imperfect and pluperfect subjunctive

These tenses are used under the same conditions as the present and perfect subjunctive, but they generally follow a different tense in the main clause. Compare the following examples:

Quiere que lo compres.
 He wants you to buy it.
Quería que lo compraras.
 He wanted you to buy it.
Espero que haya llegado.
 I hope he has arrived.
Esperaba que hubiera llegado.
 I hoped he had arrived.
Me dice que le escriba.
 He tells me to write to him.
Me dijo que le escribiera.
 He told me to write to him.
Es importante que lo haga.
 It's important that he does it.
Era importante que lo hiciese.
 It was important that he did it.

97 Sequence of tenses

The present and perfect subjunctive usually follow the present indicative, the future, the imperative, and the perfect.

The imperfect and pluperfect subjunctive usually follow the imperfect indicative, the past historic, the conditional, and the pluperfect.

Occasionally the imperfect and pluperfect subjunctive may follow a verb in the present indicative:

Siento mucho que no pudiera venir.
 I'm very sorry he could not come.
No es posible que lo supieran.
 It's not possible that they knew.
No creo que nos hubieran invitado.
 I don't think they would have invited us.

Vocabulary

viajar	to travel
el accidente	accident
poner la mesa	to set the table
darse prisa	to hurry
esperar	to hope, to wait
avisar	to warn
usar	to use
la máquina	machine
reservar	to book
la persona	person
traducir	to translate
ganar	to win
el premio	prize

Exercise 48

Translate:

1 They wanted me to travel with them.
2 I was afraid that he might have had an accident.
3 She told us to set the table.
4 I asked him to hurry up.
5 We hoped that it would not be too hot in Seville.
6 Wherever he went, he always found friends.
7 I warned him not to use that machine.
8 He called me so that I would book the rooms.
9 They were looking for a person who could translate the letter.
10 I am glad that they won the first prize.

98 The subjunctive in conditional sentences

The subjunctive is used in an "if" clause when the action of the verb is uncertain or hypothetical:

Lo compraría si tuviese el dinero.
 I would buy it if I had the money.
Acabaríamos antes si me ayudaras.
 We would finish sooner if you helped me.

When the action of the verb can be fulfilled, the indicative is used:

Lo compraré si tengo el dinero.
 I'll buy it if I have the money.
Acabaremos antes si me ayudas.
 We'll finish sooner if you help me.

When the tense of the main verb is a conditional perfect, it is usually replaced by the **-ra** form of the pluperfect subjunctive:

No le hubiera insultado si no me hubiese provocado.
 I would not have insulted him if he had not provoked me.

The future and conditional tenses are not used with **si** except when it means "whether":

No sé si vendrá.
 I don't know whether he will come.
No me dijo si lo vendería.
 He didn't tell me whether he would sell it.

Vocabulary

el perro	dog
morder (ue)	to bite
pegar	to hit
guardar	to keep
el bolsillo	pocket
divertirse (ie)	to have a good time
quedarse	to stay
más tiempo	longer
el paraguas	umbrella
mojarse	to get wet
el concierto	concert

Exercise 49

Translate:

1 I would do it, if I could.
2 If the weather is fine, I'll work in the garden.
3 The dog would not have bitten you, if you had not hit it.
4 If you asked them, they wouldn't know what to say.
5 If I saw him now, I would not speak to him.
6 You (*polite*) would not have lost the money, if you had kept it in your pocket.
7 If they came to the party, they would have a good time.
8 I shall write to you, if I have to stay there longer.
9 If you don't take an umbrella, you'll get wet.
10 I would go to the concert, if he'd come with me.

99 The subjunctive in main clauses

The subjunctive is used ...

a) in all imperatives, except the positive form of the familiar imperative:

Hable Vd., hablen Vds.
  Speak (*polite*).
No hable Vd., no hablen Vds., no hables, no habléis.
  Don't speak (*polite and familiar*).
but:
Habla, hablad.
  Speak (*familiar*).

b) to express a wish:

¡Que tenga Vd. buen viaje!
  Have a good journey!
¡Que se mejore Vd.!
  Get well soon!
¡Que sean muy felices!
  May they be very happy!

c) after the word **ojalá** ("if only," "would that ..."):

¡Ojalá pudiera verle!
  If only I could see him!
¡Ojalá ganáramos las quinielas!
  Would that we won the pools!

d) after **quizá(s), tal vez, acaso** ("perhaps"). Sometimes the indicative is used, depending on the degree of doubt:

Quizá no venga hoy.
  Perhaps he won't come today.
Acaso no lo sepan.
  Perhaps they don't know it.
Tal vez no habían oído la noticia.
  Perhaps they hadn't heard the news.

e) in certain set expressions:

Sea como sea. Be that as it may.
Sea lo que sea. Whatever it is.
Pase lo que pase. Whatever happens.
Diga lo que diga. Whatever he says.
Hagan lo que hagan. Whatever they do.

f) to translate the English "let":

Que espere. Let him wait.
Que paguen. Let them pay.

100 "May" and "might"

When they indicate possibility, "may" and "might" can be translated by any of the following expressions:

puede que, es posible que, quizá(s), tal vez: may
pudiera, era posible que, quizá(s), tal vez: might

Puede que estén trabajando.
    They may be working.
Es posible que llueva.
    It may rain.
Pensó que pudiera haber ocurrido.
    He thought that it might have happened.
Dijo que era posible que volvieran.
    He said that they might return.

When "may" and "might" are used to express permission, they are translated by the present or imperfect indicative:

¿Puedo entrar?
    May I come in?
Dijeron que podíamos jugar con ellos.
    They said we might play with them.

Vocabulary

perder	to miss (a train, boat, etc.)
estar en contacto con	to be in touch with
la fotografía	photograph
el día libre	day off
el aviso	warning (sign)

Exercise 50

Translate:

1 If only I did not have to work.
2 Perhaps he is sick.
3 We may have missed the train.
4 Let him come, if he likes.
5 If only we could have a vacation.
6 Whatever happens, I'll be in touch with you. (*pol.*)
7 May we see the photographs?
8 He said that I might have the day off.
9 Have a good time! (*pol.*)
10 Perhaps they did not see the warning sign.

101 Verbs followed by prepositions

In section 85 we have seen some common verbs that take a preposition before an infinitive. Here are some verbs that take a prepositional object.

acercarse a (to approach, to go near)
El hombre se acercó a la casa.
  The man approached the house.

asomarse a (to lean out of)
La niña se asomó a la ventana.
The girl leaned out of the window.

casarse con (to marry)
Por fin no se casó con ella.
In the end he did not marry her.

contar con (to count on, to rely on)
No puedo contar con mi hermano.
I cannot rely on my brother.

dar a (to overlook)
Los balcones daban al mar.
The balconies overlooked the sea.

depender de (to depend on)
El resultado no depende de mí.
The result does not depend on me.

despedirse de (to say good-bye to)
Vinieron a despedirse de nosotros.
They came to say good-bye to us.

dudar de (to doubt)
No dude Vd. de su palabra.
Do not doubt his word.

enamorarse de (to fall in love with)
Se enamoró de una chica muy joven.
He fell in love with a very young girl.

encontrarse con (to meet, to come across)
Me encontré con un viejo amigo.
I came across an old friend.

enterarse de (to find out, to hear about)
No me había enterado de su muerte.
I had not heard about his death.

fijarse en (to notice)
¿Se ha fijado Vd. en el sombrero de Anita?
Have you noticed Anita's hat?

ocuparse de (to attend to)
Nos ocuparemos de los invitados.
  We'll attend to the guests.

parecerse a (to resemble, to look like)
No se parece a su padre.
  He doesn't look like his father.

pensar en (to think of)
Siempre está pensando en sus hijos.
  He is always thinking of his children.

pensar de (to think of, to have an opinion on)
¿Qué piensa Vd. de esa película?
  What do you think of that film?

saber a (to taste of)
Este pastel sabe a canela.
  This cake tastes of cinnamon.

soñar con (to dream of)
Anoche soñé contigo.
  Last night I dreamed of you.

Vocabulary

el borde	edge
la ventanilla	window (of a vehicle)
concurrido (-a)	busy, crowded
el éxito	success
la obra (de teatro)	play
el compañero	colleague, companion
la buena intención	goodwill
tonto (-a)	silly
fácil	easy
el/la turista	tourist
el nombre	name
la situación	situation
el helado	ice cream
la fresa	strawberry
el lugar	place

Exercise 51

Translate:

1 Don't go near the edge.
2 He leaned out of the car window.
3 My brother is going to marry an English girl.
4 You know that you can count on me.
5 The window overlooked a very busy street.
6 The success of the play depends on the actors.
7 I have to say goodbye to my colleagues.
8 They don't doubt his goodwill.
9 Maria has fallen in love with a very silly man.
10 It's very easy to meet American tourists in Spain.
11 We have not been able to find out his name.
12 I didn't notice what she was wearing.
13 You have to attend to the drinks.
14 This house looks very much like ours.
15 He doesn't want to think of all the problems.
16 We don't know what he thinks of the situation.
17 This ice cream tastes of strawberry.
18 I was dreaming of all the places I had visited.

102 "Al" followed by infinitive

This is a very common construction in Spanish. It translates the English "on" + present participle:

Le vi al salir del hotel.

I saw him on leaving the hotel.

Al entrar en el cuarto todo el mundo dejó de hablar.

On entering the room everybody stopped talking.

It may also translate sentences with "when" and "as":

Sonrió al verme.

He smiled when he saw me.

Le saludé con la mano al entrar.

I waved at him as I came in.

Drills

26 ¿Va a venir? Is he going to come?
Puede que venga. He may come.
1 ¿Va Vd. a venderlo?
2 ¿Van a casarse?
3 ¿Van Vds. a salir?
4 ¿Va a volver?
5 ¿Van a invitarnos?
6 ¿Va Vd. a nadar?

27 *Change the verb in the future into the conditional, followed by the appropriate form of the subjunctive. Thus:*
Lo compraré si tengo dinero. I'll buy it if I have the money.
Lo compraría si tuviera dinero. I'd buy it if I had the money.

1 Vendrán si pueden.
2 Lo pediremos si lo necesitamos.
3 Comeré si tengo hambre.
4 Se lo diremos si le vemos.
5 Saldrán si no llueve.
6 Te lo daré si lo encuentro.
7 Trabajará más si le pagan bien.
8 Hablaré con ellos si vienen.

28 Se pararon cuando llegaron al puente.
They stopped when they arrived at the bridge.

Se pararon al llegar al puente.
They stopped on arriving at the bridge.

1 Se sorprendió cuando oyó la noticia. ˙
2 Gritaron cuando vieron a los policías.
3 Lloraba cuando leía la carta.
4 Me pidió la llave cuando salía.
5 Tuve miedo cuando oí un ruido.
6 Se lavaron las manos cuando terminaron.
7 Me quité el sombrero cuando entré.
8 Empezó a llover cuando llegamos a casa.

CONVERSATION

Una invitación a cenar
An invitation to dinner

El teléfono suena.
The phone rings.

Alfonso	**¡Dígame!** *Hello!*
Pilar	**¿Eres Alfonso?** *Is that Alfonso?*
Alfonso	**Sí. ¿Quién es?** *Yes. Who is it?*
Pilar	**Soy Pilar.** *It's Pilar.*
Alfonso	**¡Hola Pilar! No te había conocido. ¿Cómo estás?** *Hello Pilar! I didn't recognize your voice. How are you?*
Pilar	**Muy bien. ¿Y tú?** *Very well. And you?*
Alfonso	**Bien, gracias. ¿Querías hablar con Conchita? Ha ido a recoger a los niños al colegio.** *Fine, thanks. Did you want to speak to Conchita? She has gone to pick up the children from school.*
Pilar	**¡Ah! Bueno, no importa. La razón por la que llamo es para ver si tú y Conchita queréis venir a cenar el viernes.** *Oh! Well, it doesn't matter. The reason I'm calling is to see if you and Conchita would like to come to dinner on Friday.*

Alfonso   El viernes no podemos porque llega mi madre
de Barcelona a pasar unos días con nosotros, y
tenemos que ir al aeropuerto a las nueve de la
noche. Lo siento mucho, Pilar.
*We can't on Friday, because my mother is coming
from Barcelona to spend a few days with us, and we
have to go to the airport at nine o'clock in the
evening. I'm sorry, Pilar.*

Pilar   No te preocupes. ¿Podéis venir el sábado?
Don't worry. Can you come on Saturday?

Alfonso   El sábado, sí. Lo único es que no me gustaría
dejar sola a mi madre.
*On Saturday, yes. The only thing is I would not like
to leave my mother alone.*

Pilar   Pues, que venga también. Encantada de tener
una invitada más.
*Well, let her come, too. Delighted to have one more
guest.*

Alfonso   En ese caso, estupendo. ¿A qué hora nos
esperas?
In that case, fine. What time do you expect us?

Pilar   ¿Te parece bien a las ocho? Así tenemos tiempo
de tomar un aperitivo antes de cenar.
*Is eight o'clock all right for you? That way we'll have
time to have a drink before dinner.*

Alfonso   Muy bien. Se lo diré a Conchita. Hasta el
sábado y gracias.
*Very well. I'll tell Conchita. Till Saturday and thank
you.*

Pilar   De nada. Adiós.
Not at all. Bye.

Chapter 13

The final chapter tells you how to use certain important verbs in different contexts, and also covers special uses of:

- *"más" and "menos"*
- *"pero" and "sino"*
- *some more prepositions*
- *augmentatives and diminutives*

103 Some important verbs

It is important that you learn not only the meaning of the following verbs but also how to use them in different contexts.

asistir (to assist, to attend)
Tuve que asistir al herido.
  I had to assist the injured man.
Asistimos a una representación de Aída.
  We attended a performance of Aida.

bastar (to be enough, to suffice)
No basta decírselo.
  It's not enough to tell him.
Este pan nos basta para el desayuno.
  This bread is enough for our breakfast.

caber (to fit in)
No cabemos todos en un coche.
  We don't all fit into one car.
Este armario no cabe en esa habitación.
  This wardrobe does not fit into that room.

devolver (to return, to give back)
Me ha devuelto mi carta.
  He has returned my letter.
Nos devolvieron el dinero.
  They refunded our money.

echar (to throw, to pour)
Eché la carta al fuego.
  I threw the letter on the fire.
Echó el té en la taza.
  She poured the tea in the cup.

faltar (to lack, to be missing)
No le falta inteligencia.
  He doesn't lack intelligence.
Faltan dos páginas en este libro.
  There are two pages missing in this book.

hacer falta (to need)
No hace falta ir más lejos.
  There is no need to go any further.
Me hace falta más gasolina.
  I need more gas.

meter (to put in, to insert)
Metió la llave en la cerradura.
  He put the key in the lock.
Me metí la mano en el bolsillo.
  I put my hand in my pocket.

quedar (to remain, to have left)
Quedan cuatro lecciones.
  Four lessons remain.
Me quedan cuarenta dólares.
  I have forty dollars left.

quitar(se) (to take away, to take off)
Le quitaron el pasaporte.
  They took his passport.
Me quité los zapatos.
  I took off my shoes.

sobrar (to have more than enough, to have to spare)
Sobran candidatos para ese trabajo.
  There are more than enough candidates for that job.
¿Te sobra algo de dinero?
  Do you have any money to spare?

tocar (to touch, to play an instrument)
No toque Vd. la pintura.
  Don't touch the paint.
Toca la guitarra maravillosamente.
  He plays the guitar beautifully.

tomar (to take, to have food or drink)
Tomó al niño en sus brazos.
  He took the child in his arms.
Vamos a tomar un café.
  Let's have coffee.

Vocabulary

la gente	people
el entierro	funeral
la cantidad	amount
la harina	flour
la caja	box
el maletero	car trunk
prestar	to lend
la pelota	ball
el estante	shelf
el ayudante	helper
la silla	chair
la chaqueta	jacket
el huevo	egg
la tortilla	omelet
la seda	silk
el violín	violin
firmar	to sign

Exercise 52

Translate:

1 Many people attended the funeral.
2 This amount of flour will be enough.
3 That box doesn't fit in the trunk of the car.
4 I want to return the magazine he lent me.
5 He threw the ball to the children.
6 I am going to pour the wine.
7 They lack experience.
8 There are five books missing from this shelf.
9 We need more helpers.
10 They will put all the clothes in one suitcase.
11 How many days do you have left?
12 He will take away these chairs.
13 May I take off my jacket?
14 There are more than enough eggs to make the omelet.
15 It's very pleasant to touch silk.
16 He would like to play the violin.
17 He took the pen and signed the letter.
18 They like to have wine with their meal.

104 "Más" and "menos"

We have already seen these two words in the comparatives **más que** (more than) and **menos que** (less than). But when "more than" and "less than" are followed by a numeral, they are translated by **más de** and **menos de**. For example:

Hay más de quinientos alumnos en esa escuela.
There are more than five hundred pupils in that school.
He pagado menos de trescientas pesetas.
I have paid less than three hundred pesetas.

In the negative, **que** replaces **de** and **no ... más que** is translated by "only":

No tengo más que un hermano.
I only have one brother.
No hay más que tres manzanas.
There are only three apples.

When **más de** and **menos de** are followed by a clause, the forms **el que, la que, los que, las que,** must be used. If no definite noun is referred to, **lo que** is used. Therefore:

Tenemos más comida de la que necesitamos.
We have more food than we need.
Es más inteligente de lo que parece.
He is more intelligent than he looks.

105 "Tan" and "tal"

Both words translate the English "such," but **tan** precedes an adjective where **tal(es)** precedes a noun:

Es un libro tan interesante.
It's such an interesting book.
No conozco a tal hombre.
I don't know such a man.

Tan is also used in exclamations:

¡Qué casa tan bonita!
What a lovely house!
¡Qué día tan horrible!
What a horrible day!

The adjective **semejante** can also translate "such":

No diga Vd. semejante cosa.
Don't say such a thing.

106 "Pero" and "sino"

Although "but" is generally translated by **pero**, remember to use **sino** after a negative statement when "but" introduces a clause that is contrary to the first statement:

Este regalo no es para mi madre, sino para mi hermana.
This present is not for my mother, but for my sister.
No he pedido carne, sino pescado.
I ordered fish, but not meat.

Vocabulary

heredar	to inherit
el collar	necklace
feo	ugly
el edificio	building
aburrido	boring
listo	clever

Exercise 53

Translate:

1 He has inherited more than twenty million pesetas.
2 I cannot sell it for less than ten thousand pesetas.
3 We have lived in Madrid more than fifteen years.
4 I shall do it in less than five minutes.
5 He had never seen such a beautiful necklace.
6 What an ugly building!
7 He wouldn't do such a thing.
8 I find such books very boring.
9 That is not my brother, but my cousin.
10 They don't have a dog, but they have two cats.
11 He has more money than he says.
12 They are more clever than you think.
13 What a good idea!
14 It is such a long journey!

107 Prepositions

Here is a list of the most common simple and compound prepositions. **Por** and **para** are not included, since they have been dealt with in chapter 10.

a (to, at) Used in expressions of time and a few set phrases such as: **a la mesa** "at the table," **a la puerta** "at the door."
Van a la playa.
> They go to the beach.

Te veré a las ocho.
> I'll see you at eight.

Nos sentamos a la mesa.
> We sat at the table.

ante (before) Meaning "in the presence of," "faced with."
Ante ese problema, no supo que hacer.
> Faced with that problem, he didn't know what to do.

Se presentó ante el tribunal.
> He appeared before the court.

antes de (before time)
Llegaremos antes de las cuatro.
> We shall arrive before four o'clock.

bajo (under)
Trabaja bajo su dirección.
> He works under him.

debajo de (under = underneath)
Encontré la sortija debajo del sillón.
> I found the ring under the armchair.

con (with)
Iremos con Juan.
> We'll go with John.

¿Quiere Vd. venir conmigo?
> Do you want to come with me?

contra (against)
Ponga Vd. esa silla contra la pared.
> Put that chair against the wall.

de (of, from, about)
La casa de Conchita.
  Conchita's house.
Estamos hablando de Vd.
  We are talking about you.
Trabajo de nueve a dos.
  I work from nine till two.

delante de (in front of)
Andaba delante de mí.
  He was walking in front of me.

desde (from) This is more emphatic than **de**.
Desde la ventana se ve el mar.
  From the window one can see the sea.

después de (after = time)
Después de cenar daremos un paseo.
  After dinner we shall go for a walk.

detrás de (behind)
El garaje está detrás de la casa.
  The garage is behind the house.

en (in, on, at)
El regalo está en la caja.
  The present is in the box.
La comida está en la mesa.
  The food is on the table.
Estarán en casa todo el día.
  They will be at home all day.

encima de (on top of, over)
La maleta está encima del armario.
  The suitcase is on top of the wardrobe.

enfrente de (opposite)
La farmacia está enfrente del banco.
  The drugstore is opposite the bank.

entre (between)
Podemos pagar los gastos entre nosotros.
  We can pay the expenses between us.

hacia (towards, about = of time)
El niño vino hacia nosotros.
The boy came towards us.
Volveremos hacia el veinte de septiembre.
We shall come back towards the 20th of September.

hasta (until, as far as)
Durmió hasta las once.
He slept until eleven.
Me acompañó hasta la parada de autobús.
He accompanied me as far as the bus stop.

según (according to)
Según el hombre del tiempo, va a llover.
According to the weatherman, it's going to rain.

sin (without)
No podemos viajar sin pasaporte.
We cannot travel without a passport.

sobre (on, upon, about)
Las cartas están sobre la mesa.
The letters are on the table.
Tenemos que hablar sobre ese tema.
We have to talk about that subject.

tras (after)
El perro corrió tras la pelota.
The dog ran after the ball.

Vocabulary

espléndido	generous, fantastic
la fila	line, row
el juez	judge
la cama	bed
la zapatería	shoe store
la panadería	bakery
el piso	floor
probar	to try, to test
el sofá	sofa
el paquete	parcel
el escritorio	desk

Exercise 54

Translate:

1 The man was sleeping under a tree.
2 He wrote to me from Córdoba.
3 After the theater, we went to his house.
4 He is very generous with his friends.
5 We waited at the door, but he did not come.
6 According to his father, he is very sick.
7 There was a long line of cars in front of me.
8 He had to appear before the judge.
9 They left without paying for the drink.
10 He put the suitcase under the bed.
11 There is a shoe store opposite the bakery.
12 I won't see you until Sunday.
13 The elevator stopped between the two floors.
14 I want to try it before buying it.
15 We will start walking towards the station.
16 They will have to go on the bus.
17 The book has fallen behind the sofa.
18 I will leave the package on top of the desk.

108 Augmentatives and diminutives

Certain augmentative and diminutive endings are added to nouns to qualify their meaning. Since the use of these terminations can present considerable difficulties without a thorough knowledge of the language, you should use adjectives instead.

a) Augmentatives:

-ón, -azo, -acho, -ote express largeness and may also imply some degree of awkwardness or ugliness.

un hombrón a big man
unos ojazos big eyes
una mujerona a big woman

b) Diminutives:

-ito, -ico, -illo, -uelo express smallness and sometimes fondness on the part of the speaker:

un perrito a little dog
un corrillo a small circle of people
un polluelo a chick

Many augmentatives and diminutives have established themselves as words in their own right:

ventana (window)	→ ventanilla (window of a vehicle)
silla (chair)	→ sillín (saddle), sillón (armchair)
puerta (door)	→ portezuela (door of a vehicle)
cera (wax)	→ cerillas (matches)
caja (box)	→ cajón (drawer)
camisa (shirt)	→ camisón (nightgown)
pan (bread)	→ panecillo (roll)
niebla (fog)	→ neblina (mist)

109 Idiomatic uses of certain verbs

Note the underlined idiomatic uses and meanings which are additional to that given against the principal (infinitive) translation.

- caer to fall

La pobre mujer cayó enferma y murió a las dos semanas.
The poor woman fell sick and died two weeks later.

Es un hombre que me cae mal.
He is a man I dislike.

Ese vestido te cae muy bien.
That dress fits you very well.

No han caído en la cuenta.
They haven't "caught on."

- **dar** to give

Vamos a <u>dar un paseo</u> / <u>Vamos a dar una vuelta</u>.
Let's go for a walk.

Las dos hermanas <u>se dieron un abrazo</u>.
The two sisters embraced each other.

Al ver al ladrón, <u>di un grito</u>.
On seeing the burglar, I screamed.

Las ventanas de los dormitorios <u>dan a una pequeña plaza</u>.
The bedroom windows overlook a little square.

No olvides <u>dar de comer</u> al perro.
Don't forget to feed the dog.

No <u>se dio cuenta</u> del error.
He didn't realize the mistake.

No puedo seguir jugando, me <u>doy por vencido</u>.
I can't go on playing, I give up.

Es tarde, tenemos que <u>dar la vuelta</u>.
It's late, we have to turn back.

Voy a <u>darle los buenos días</u> a tu madre.
I am going to say good morning to your mother.

Tenemos que <u>darnos prisa</u> o no llegaremos a tiempo.
We have to hurry or we won't be on time.

Han ido a <u>dar parte</u> del robo a la policía.
They have gone to report the theft to the police.

Al despedirse, <u>se dieron la mano</u>.
As they said good-bye, they shook hands.

Podemos tomar vino blanco o tinto, <u>lo mismo me da</u>.
We can have white or red wine, it's all the same to me.

- **dejar(se)** to allow, to leave behind

Sus padres no <u>le dejan salir</u>.
His parents won't let him go out.

Hemos <u>dejado</u> el coche en el aparcamiento.
We have left the car in the parking lot.

Me <u>dejé</u> el paraguas en el taxi.
I left my umbrella in the taxi.

- **dejar de** to give up, to stop

¿Cuándo vas a <u>dejar de</u> trabajar?
When are you going to stop working?

No <u>dejes de</u> llamarme.
Call me.

- **despedir(se)** to dismiss, to say good-bye (to)

Han <u>despedido</u> a cien empleados.
They have dismissed one hundred employees.

Carmen vino a <u>despedirme</u> al aeropuerto.
Carmen came to see me off at the airport.

- **echar** to throw

<u>Echa</u> estos periódicos a la basura.
Throw these newspapers in the bin.

Tenemos que <u>echar estas cartas</u> antes de las cuatro.
We have to mail these letters before four o'clock.

No debes <u>echar la culpa</u> a Juan.
You must not blame Juan.

Cuando vi el autobús, <u>eché a correr</u>, pero no pude cogerlo.
When I saw the bus, I started to run, but I couldn't catch it.

Me gusta vivir en Nueva York, pero <u>echo de menos</u> el clima del Mediterráneo.
I like living in New York, but I miss the Mediterranean climate.

Siempre está dispuesto a <u>echar una mano</u>.
He is always ready to lend a hand.

No olvides <u>echar la llave</u> a la puerta.
Don't forget to lock the door.

- **llevar(se)** to carry, to take, to wear

Tuvimos que <u>llevarle</u> al médico.
We had to take him to the doctor.

No me gusta <u>llevar</u> sombrero.
I don't like to wear a hat.

Los dos hermanos <u>se llevan</u> muy bien.
The two brothers get along very well.

Mi marido <u>me lleva</u> cuatro años.
My husband is four years older than I.

No le gusta cuando <u>le llevan la contraria</u>.
He doesn't like it when they contradict him.

Viven en el campo y <u>llevan una vida</u> muy tranquila.
They live in the country and they lead a very quiet life.

- **valer** to be worth, to cost

¿Cuánto <u>vale</u> el alquiler del coche?
How much is the car rental?

<u>Más vale</u> ir directamente al hotel.
It's better to go straight to the hotel.

<u>No vale la pena</u> esperar.
It's not worth waiting.

Drills

29 ¿Necesita Vd. el paraguas? Do you need the umbrella?
No, no me hace falta. No, I don't need it.

¿Necesitan Vds. sellos? Do you need stamps?
No, no nos hacen falta. No, we don't need them.

1 ¿Necesita Carmen el coche?
2 ¿Necesitan Vds. el pasaporte?
3 ¿Necesita Vd. estas cajas?
4 ¿Necesitan ellos ayuda?
5 ¿Necesita Ramón las gafas?
6 ¿Necesitan Vds. otra maleta?

30 Ha firmado Vd. la carta? Have you signed the letter?
No puedo firmarla todavía. I cannot sign it yet.

1 ¿Han devuelto Vds. el dinero?
2 ¿Ha metido Vd. la ropa en la maleta?
3 ¿Han echado ellos las postales?
4 ¿Se ha quitado Vd. los zapatos?
5 ¿Han tomado Vds. vino?
6 ¿Ha pagado Carlos la cuenta?

31 *Fill in the blanks with the appropriate preposition from the column on the right.*

1 Trabajaré _____ las cinco.	en
2 Nos escribirá _____ Sevilla.	sin
3 El hotel está _____ la playa.	hacia
4 He dejado la maleta _____ la cama.	antes de
5 _____ los dos podemos mover el armario.	enfrente de
6 No puedes salir _____ abrigo.	desde
7 Queremos hablar _____ el gerente.	encima de
8 No podré llegar _____ las diez.	con
9 Te esperaremos _____ casa.	entre
10 Los niños corrieron _____ su padre.	hasta

CONVERSATION

En el tren
On the train

Felipe ¿Perdone, está ocupado este asiento?
Excuse me. Is this seat taken?

Lolita No, no creo.
No, I don't think so.

Felipe Menos mal. Creí que no iba a encontrar sitio.
El tren está casi lleno.
*Thank goodness. I thought I wasn't going to find a
place. The train is almost full.*

Lolita Es verdad. Nunca he visto tanta gente en este
tren.
*It's true. I have never seen so many people on this
train.*

Felipe ¿Le importa que abra un poco la ventanilla?
Tengo mucho calor.
*Do you mind if I open the window a little? I am very
hot.*

Lolita Ábrala. Yo también necesito un poco de
aire fresco.
Open it. I need a little fresh air, too.

Felipe ¿Quiere Vd. un pitillo?
Would you like a cigarette?

Lolita No, gracias. No fumo.
No thanks. I don't smoke.

Felipe ¿Le molesta que fume yo?
Do you mind if I smoke?

Lolita En absoluto. Aunque no fumo, me gusta el olor
del tabaco.
*Not at all. Although I don't smoke, I like the smell of
tobacco.*

Felipe **¿No ha fumado Vd. nunca?**
Have you ever smoked?

Lolita **Sí, pero lo dejé hace dos años.**
Yes, but I gave it up two years ago.

Felipe **Yo llevo mucho tiempo tratando de dejarlo, pero no lo consigo. Me falta fuerza de voluntad.**
I have been trying for a long time to give it up, but I am not succeeding. I lack willpower.

Lolita **Bueno, parece que nos ponemos en marcha. ¿Va Vd. a Segovia?**
Well, it looks as if we are moving. Are you going to Segovia?

Felipe **Sí. Tengo que visitar una fábrica allí. No voy a estar más que dos días. Y ¿Vd.?**
Yes. I have to visit a factory there. I am only going to stay a couple of days. And you?

Lolita **Yo también voy a Segovia, a pasar una semana con unos amigos. ¡Ay, qué rabia! He olvidado comprar algo para leer en el viaje.**
I am going to Segovia, too, to spend a week with some friends. Oh, no! I have forgotten to buy something to read on the journey.

Felipe **¿Quiere Vd. esta revista?**
Would you like this magazine?

Lolita **Si a Vd. no le hace falta de momento, me gustaría verla. Gracias.**
If you don't need it for the moment, I'd like to see it. Thanks.

Revision – 4

Exercise 1

Translate:

1 They must have gone out.
2 She could neither read nor write.
3 We ought to wait a few more minutes.
4 Can you (*pol.sing.*) tell me the time?
5 He was afraid because he could not swim.
6 You (*fam.sing.*) should invite her to dinner.
7 They owe me two thousand pesetas.
8 You (*fam.pl.*) must decide what you want to do.

Exercise 2

Put the verbs in brackets into the correct form of the present subjunctive:

1 Quiere que nosotros [ir] con él.
2 Necesito que ella me [ayudar] en la cocina.
3 Es preferible que ellos [quedarse] en casa.
4 Le han prohibido que [salir].
5 No quieren que yo lo [saber].
6 Sentimos que usted no [poder] venir.
7 Es probable que [llover] hoy.
8 Me alegro de que vosotros [tener] éxito.
9 No le gusta que su hija [jugar] con esos niños.
10 No quiero que tú [llegar] tarde.
11 Se lo diremos cuando le [ver].
12 Esperaremos hasta que él [venir].
13 Dígale a Paco que me [llamar].
14 Dudo que ellos [tener] suficiente dinero.
15 No debes permitirle que lo [hacer].
16 ¿Hay alguien que me [acompañar]?

Exercise 3

*Use the verbs in brackets in the following phrases to make commands using the **tú** form:*

1 [Esperar] un momento.
2 [Sentarse] aquí.
3 [Darle] las llaves.
4 [Hacer] el café.
5 No [pedir] más caramelos.
6 [Tener] cuidado.
7 No [traer] al perro.
8 [Venir] pasado mañana.

Exercise 4

*Use the verbs in brackets in the following phrases to make commands using the **vosotros** form:*

1 [Limpiar] vuestra habitación.
2 No [volver] a casa tarde.
3 [Comer] en la cafetería.
4 [Acostarse] temprano.
5 No [decirle] que estoy enfermo.
6 No [ir] a España en agosto.
7 [Escribir] vuestro nombre aquí.
8 No [telefonearme] antes de las once.

Exercise 5

Put the verbs in brackets into either of the correct forms of the subjunctive:

1 Nos extrañó que él no [estar] allí.
2 Le dije que me lo [enviar] al hotel.
3 Nos pidió que le [perdonar].
4 No quisieron que yo [ir] al aeropuerto.
5 Te lo diríamos si lo [saber].

6 Ojalá tú [poder] venir de vacaciones conmigo.
7 Era importante que ellos [firmar] ese documento.
8 Podrían comer en el jardín si [hacer] mejor tiempo.
9 Yo no estaría aquí si eso [ser] verdad.
10 Pedro no te daría dinero aunque tú lo [necesitar].
11 Nos aconsejó que no [vender] la casa.
12 Me dijo que [traer] el pasaporte.

Exercise 6

Your friend Paco, whom you haven't seen for some time, calls you to arrange a meeting. Answer him in Spanish.

Paco	Te llamo porque hace mucho tiempo que no nos vemos.
Usted	I know. I've had a lot of work.
Paco	¿Por qué no vamos a cenar mañana?
Usted	I am sorry. I don't have any free evenings this week.
Paco	Entonces, díme cuándo podemos vernos.
Usted	Saturday of next week?
Paco	¡Vale! ¿Dónde quieres que nos veamos?
Usted	Come to my house at 8 P.M. We'll have a drink and then decide where to go for dinner.
Paco	¿No crees que debiéramos reservar una mesa? Todos los restaurantes van a estar llenos.
Usted	Perhaps you are right. Do you want me to make a reservation in a restaurant not far from where I live?
Paco	Muy bien. Te lo dejo a ti. Nos vemos en tu casa. Adiós. Hasta el sábado.
Usted	Good-bye, and thank you for calling.

Exercise 7

*Complete the following sentences using the appropriate idiom with the verb **tener** in the correct form:*

1 Me voy a bañar en la piscina porque _____
2 No quería quedarse sola en casa porque _____
3 Se puso la chaqueta porque _____
4 Vamos a tomar una cerveza porque _____
5 Se acostaron temprano porque _____
6 No pudimos esperar más porque _____
7 Nos reímos mucho con la película porque _____
8 No comieron nada para el desayuno porque _____
9 No ganaré nunca la lotería porque _____

Exercise 8

Translate:

1 That coat doesn't fit you (*fam.sing.*) very well.
2 He has become sick and he has been taken to the hospital.
3 We decided to go for a short walk.
4 Hurry up (*fam.sing.*) The train leaves at 9:45.
5 He never says good morning to me.
6 They started to go up the mountain, but they soon gave up.
7 I have come to say good-bye.
8 We cannot blame anybody.
9 You (*fam.sing.*) must miss Pedro, he was a good friend of yours.
10 Could you (*fam.sing.*) lend me a hand with these packages?
11 Did you (*pol.sing.*) lock the suitcase before leaving the room?
12 I don't want you to contradict me.
13 We get along very well, we never argue.
14 It's better to take the umbrella, it may rain.

Exercise 9

Translate:

1 What a lot of people!
2 The man we saw yesterday is her husband.
3 Whose magazines are these?
4 Which seat do you (*fam.sing.*) prefer?
5 What a boring movie!
6 The woman for whom she works is an actress.
7 How difficult it is to see him!
8 The room in which we slept overlooked the sea.
9 Those who need more information may ask that lady.
10 You (*fam.sing.*) must show me the present he has given you.
11 It is we who have to send it.
12 He didn't want to go, which surprised me.
13 I asked him who had come, but he didn't tell me.
14 That is the woman whose house they have bought.
15 They are friends with whom I am always in touch.
16 What we don't understand is why he hasn't written.

Reading practice

The following extracts from works by modern Spanish authors each have an English translation on the facing page. Refer to this as little as possible during your first reading of the Spanish, then go through the piece again, noting constructions and vocabulary.

Los Españolitos de Alsemberg

A Santi se le hizo muy cuesta arriba vivir en la casa de los Dufour.
Y no es que no le tratasen bien, no. Al contrario, tanto Raymond
Dufour como su mujer, Arlette, hicieron desde el principio todo lo
posible para que Santi se sintiese a sus anchas y para que no le
faltase nada de cuanto podía necesitar o desear.

Durante varios días, Arlette y Raymond Dufour habían estado
hablando de como sería el niño español que había de venir a su
casa y era cosa decidida que ellos harían todo lo posible para tratarle
con comprensión y cariño. Vivían en una casa amplia, muy
bonita, de dos pisos, como un chalet, en el barrio de Forest, cerca
de un parque lleno de flores y de campos de tenis y de fútbol, con
pequeños tio-vivos y toboganes y columpios. Era un parque alegre
y sonriente que estaba todo el día lleno de niños, de escolares, de
niñeras y de palomas. Para Santi habían hecho empapelar y
amueblar especialmente una habitación muy simpática, luminosa,
con una pequeña chimenea, estanterías llenas de libros españoles
y muchas pinturas y fotografías de España y banderines y juguetes.

Pero nada más entrar en la habitación, aquella primera noche,
Santi supo que no se iba a encontrar a gusto. Se sintió emocionado
al observar el cariño con que los Dufour habían preparado todo
aquello para él y captó la mirada expectante de Madame Dufour
que parecía preguntarse, con angustia, si aquello le gustaba o no.

Santi era cortés y tenía un gran sentido de gratitud. Dijo que todo
era muy bonito y que gracias. Madame Dufour le abrazó y habló
con su marido y Raymond Dufour dijo:

—Dice que quiere que seas feliz con nosotros, Santiago.

Ella le trajo un vaso de leche y unas galletas y aunque Santi no
tenía ninguna gana de tomar nada, tomó el vaso de leche por
complacerla. Las galletas no, porque realmente no podía.

La cama era cómoda y limpia. Raymond Dufour había depositado
la maleta de Santi al lado de la cama y Santi no sabía qué hacer.
Bostezó dos veces adrede – aunque estaba realmente muy cansado;
las emociones del día le habían agotado – y Madame Dufour
pronunció unas palabras en francés. Monsieur Dufour dijo:

—Duerme bien, Santiago. Mañana iremos de compras y también
iremos en coche de paseo por Bruselas para que veas la ciudad.
Luego almorzaremos en un restaurante, compras el regalo que
quieras para tu hermana, e iremos a verla. ¿Te parece?

"Los Españolitos de Alsemberg" is taken from "El otro árbol de
  Guernica" (The other tree of Guernica) by Luis de Castresana
  (born 1925).

The Spanish Children of Alsemberg

Santi found it very hard to live in the Dufours' house. It wasn't that they did not treat him well. On the contrary, from the beginning both Raymond Dufour and his wife Arlette did all they could to make Santi feel at ease and to give him everything that he needed or wished.

For several days, Arlette and Raymond Dufour had been talking of what the little Spanish boy who was coming to their house might be like, and they decided that they would do everything in their power to treat him with understanding and love. They lived in a big, two story house, very pretty, like a villa, in the Forest district, near a park full of flowers, with tennis courts and a soccer field, with small merry-go-rounds and slides and swings. It was a cheerful, jolly park that was always full of children, schoolboys, nannies, and pigeons. They had had a room papered and furnished especially for Santi, a very pleasant, light room, with a small fireplace, bookshelves full of Spanish books and many pictures and photographs of Spain, and pennants and toys.

But as soon as Santi entered the room, that first night, he knew that he wasn't going to feel happy there. He was touched by the love with which the Dufours had prepared all that for him, and he was aware of the expectant look of Madame Dufour, who seemed to be wondering, anxiously, whether he liked all that or not.

Santi was polite, and he had a great sense of gratitude. He said that everything was very nice and he thanked them. Madame Dufour hugged him and spoke to her husband, and Raymond Dufour said: "She says that she wants you to be happy with us, Santiago."

She brought him a glass of milk and some cookies, and, although Santi didn't feel like having anything, he drank the milk just to please her. He didn't eat the cookies, he really couldn't.

The bed was comfortable and clean. Raymond Dufour had left Santi's suitcase by the bed and Santi didn't know what to do next. He yawned twice on purpose – although he really was very tired; the emotions of the day had made him feel exhausted – and Madame Dufour said a few words in French. Monsieur Dufour said: "Sleep well, Santiago. Tomorrow we will go shopping, and we will also go for a ride in the car around Brussels so that you can see the city. Then we will have lunch in a restaurant, you buy any present you like for your sister, and we will go to visit her. Does that suit you?"

Primera Memoria

—Te domaremos — me dijo mi abuela, apenas llegué a la isla.

Tenía doce años, y por primera vez comprendí que me quedaría allí para siempre. Mi madre murió cuatro años atrás y Mauricia – la vieja aya que me cuidaba – estaba impedida por una enfermedad. Mi abuela se hacía cargo definitivamente de mí, estaba visto.

El día que llegué a la isla, hacía mucho viento en la ciudad. Unos rótulos medio desprendidos tableteaban sobre las puertas de las tiendas. Me llevó la abuela a un hotel oscuro, que olía a humedad y lejía. Mi habitación daba a un pequeño patio, por un lado, y, por el otro, a un callejón, tras cuya embocadura se divisaba un paseo donde se mecían las palmeras sobre un pedazo de mar plomizo. La cama de hierro forjado, muy complicada, me amedrentó como un animal desconocido. La abuela dormía en la habitación contigua, y de madrugada me desperté sobresaltada – como me ocurría a menudo y busqué, tanteando, con el brazo extendido, el interruptor de la luz de la mesilla. Recuerdo bien el frío de la pared estucada, y la pantalla rosa de la lámpara. Me estuve muy quieta, sentada en la cama, mirando recelosa alrededor, asombrada del retorcido mechón de mi propio cabello que resaltaba oscuramente contra mi hombro. Habituándome a la penumbra, localicé, uno a uno, los desconchados de la pared, las grandes manchas del techo, y sobre todo, las sombras enzarzadas de la cama, como serpientes, dragones, o misteriosas figuras que apenas me atrevía a mirar. Incliné el cuerpo cuanto pude hacia la mesilla, para coger el vaso de agua, y entonces, en el vértice de la pared, descubrí una hilera de hormigas que trepaba por el muro. Solté el vaso, que se rompió al caer, y me hundí de nuevo entre las sábanas, tapándome la cabeza. No me decidía a sacar ni una mano, y así estuve mucho rato, mordiéndome los labios y tratando de ahuyentar las despreciables lágrimas. Me parece que tuve miedo. Acaso pensé que estaba completamente sola, y, como buscando algo que no sabía.

Taken from the novel "Primera Memoria" by Ana Maria Matute (born 1926).

First Memory

"We will tame you" my grandmother told me as soon as I arrived on the island.

I was twelve years old, and for the first time I realized that I would be staying there forever. My mother had died four years earlier, and Mauricia, the old nanny who had looked after me, was now an invalid. My grandmother was going to take charge of me forever, that was clear.

The day I arrived on the island, it was very windy in the city. Some placards hanging loose were rattling on the doors of the stores. Grandmother took me to a gloomy hotel that smelled of dampness and bleach. My room overlooked a small yard on one side, and on the other side, an alley at the end of which one could see a promenade with palm trees swaying over a leaden sea. The intricate design of the wrought iron bed frightened me like an unknown animal. Grandmother was sleeping in the room next to mine, and at dawn I woke up startled, as I often did, and I stretched out my arm groping for the switch of the bedside lamp. I remember well the coldness of the stuccoed wall and the pink lampshade. I remained very still, sitting up in bed, looking around me suspiciously, fascinated by a curly lock of my hair resting darkly on my shoulder. As I got used to the dimness, I noticed, one by one, the chips on the wall, the large stains on the ceiling, and, above all, the twisted shadows of the bed, like snakes, dragons, or mysterious figures that I hardly dared look at. I leaned over to the bedside table, to pick up a glass of water, and then, in the corner of the room, I discovered a row of ants climbing up the wall. I dropped the glass, which broke, and sunk back between the sheets, covering my head. I did not dare show even one hand and I remained that way a long time, biting my lips and trying to hold back the despicable tears. I think I was afraid. Perhaps I thought that I was completely alone, and I was looking for something I did not know.

El Coronel no tiene quien le escriba

El viernes siguiente volvió a las lanchas. Y como todos los viernes regresó a su casa sin la carta esperada. 'Ya hemos cumplido con esperar', le dijo esa noche su mujer. 'Se necesita tener esa paciencia de buey que tú tienes para esperar una carta durante quince años'. El coronel se metió en la hamaca a leer los periódicos.

—Hay que esperar el turno — dijo. — Nuestro número es el mil ochocientos veintitrés.

—Desde que estamos esperando, ese número ha salido dos veces en la lotería — replicó la mujer.

El coronel leyó, como siempre, desde la primera página hasta la última, incluso los avisos. Pero esta vez no se concentró. Durante la lectura pensó en su pensión de veterano. Diecinueve años antes, cuando el congreso promulgó la ley, se inició un proceso de justificación que duró ocho años. Luego necesitó seis años más para hacerse incluir en el escalafón. Esa fue la última carta que recibió el coronel.

Terminó después del toque de queda. Cuando iba a apagar la lámpara cayó en la cuenta de que su mujer estaba despierta.

— ¿Tienes todavía aquel recorte?

La mujer pensó.

—Sí. Debe estar con los otros papeles.

Salió del mosquitero y extrajo del armario un cofre de madera con un paquete de cartas ordenadas por las fechas y aseguradas con una cinta elástica. Localizó un anuncio de una agencia de abogados que se comprometía a una gestión activa de las pensiones de guerra.

—Desde que estoy con el tema de que cambies de abogado ya hubiéramos tenido tiempo hasta de gastarnos la plata — dijo la mujer, entregando a su marido el recorte de periódico. — Nada sacamos con que nos la metan en el cajón como a los indios.

El coronel leyó el recorte fechado dos años antes. Lo guardó en el bolsillo de la camisa colgada detrás de la puerta.

—Lo malo es que para el cambio de abogado se necesita dinero.

—Nada de eso — decidió la mujer. — Se les escribe diciendo que descuenten lo que sea de la misma pensión cuando la cobren. Es la única manera de que se interesen en el asunto.

Así que el sábado en la tarde el coronel fue a visitar a su abogado.

Taken from the novel "El Coronel no tiene quien le escriba" by the Colombian author Gabriel García Márquez (born 1928).

No one writes to the Colonel

The following Friday he went down to the launches again. And, as on every Friday, he returned home without the long awaited letter. "We've waited long enough," his wife told him that night. "One must have the patience of an ox, as you do, to wait for a letter for fifteen years." The colonel got into his hammock to read the newspapers.

"We have to wait our turn," he said. "Our number is 1823."

"Since we've been waiting, that number has come up twice in the lottery," his wife replied.

The colonel read, as usual, from the first page to the last, including the advertisements. But this time he didn't concentrate. During his reading, he thought about his veteran's pension. Nineteen years earlier, when Congress passed the law, it took him eight years to prove his claim. Then it took him six more years to get himself included on the rolls. That was the last letter the colonel had received.

He finished after curfew sounded. When he went to turn off the lamp, he realized that his wife was awake.

"Do you still have that clipping?"

The woman thought.

"Yes. It must be with the other papers."

She got out of her mosquito netting and took a wooden box out of the wardrobe, with a bundle of letters arranged by dates and held together by a rubber band. She found the advertisement of a legal firm that promised quick action on war pensions.

"We could have spent the money in the time I've wasted trying to convince you to change lawyers," the woman said, handing her husband the newspaper clipping. "We won't get anything out of it if they put the money in our coffin as they do with the Indians."

The colonel read the clipping, dated two years before. He put it in the pocket of his jacket that was hanging behind the door.

"The problem is that to change lawyers you need money."

"Not at all," said the woman decisively. "You write to them telling them to discount whatever it may be from the pension itself when they collect it. It's the only way they'll work with interest on the case."

So, Saturday afternoon the colonel went to see his lawyer.

Un pueblo de sueño

Llegamos a Sevilla y fuimos a un hotel de una plaza con grandes palmeras.

Nos han instalado en habitaciones del piso bajo, cuyas ventanas dan a un gran patio con una fuente en medio, enlozado de mármol blanco, y rodeado de una arcada también de mármol.

El cuarto me ha parecido húmedo y frío, como sitio donde no entra el sol y que no tiene chimenea ni nada para calentarlo.

Mi marido y yo cenamos a las ocho, y después de cenar fuimos a dar una vuelta por el pueblo.

En la calle de las Sierpes he llamado la atención. ¿Por qué? Realmente no llevaba nada llamativo. Quizá encontraban en mí cierto aire exótico.

Dimos varias vueltas a esta calle estrecha tortuosa, y luego nos sentamos en un café.

Al extranjero que viene a Sevilla lo que le choca primero son los muchos hombres que andan por la calle y las pocas mujeres.

En España he oído decir que se considera a las mujeres de Sevilla como muy bonitas, pero a mí, si tengo que decir la verdad y juzgar por las de la calle, no me han llamada la atención. En el Norte y en Madrid he visto tipos más bellos y con el mismo carácter meridional.

Realmente, en España no hay gran diferencia entre la gente del Norte y la del Sur; no pasa como en Italia; aquí, por lo que veo, apenas se distingue un andaluz de un vascongado y un gallego de un catalán.

Desde la ventana del café veo, un poco cansada, como se agita la multitud de hombres que llenan la calle. Hay muchos que deben de ser toreros, porque llevan coleta como los chinos, una coleta pequeña retorcida para arriba que parece el rabito de un cerdo.

Entre algunas de estas caras anémicas, borrosas, de poca expresión, hay tipos de hombres altos, con aire enérgico, que me recuerdan las esculturas romanas del Museo de Florencia. Muchos se apoyan en las paredes en actitud de languidez y de pereza.

—¿Estás cansada o damos otro paseo? — me ha preguntado Juan.

—No, vamos.

Hemos salido del café. Son cerca de las diez de la noche y muchas tiendas están abiertas. Sigue el eterno ir y venir de la gente.

Taken and adapted from the novel "El mundo es ansí" by
Pío Baroja (1872–1956).

A dream town

We arrived in Seville and went to a hotel in a square with big palm trees.

They put us in rooms on the ground floor, whose windows overlook a large inner court with a fountain in the middle, a white marble floor, and surrounded by a marble arcade.

The room seemed to me damp and cold, a place where the sun never enters and which has no fireplace or anything to warm it up.

My husband and I had dinner at eight, and after dinner we went for a walk around the town.

In Sierpes Street people were looking at me. Why? I was not wearing anything showy. Perhaps they found something exotic about me.

We walked up and down this narrow, winding street, and then went to sit in a café.

The first thing that strikes the foreigner who comes to Seville is how many men there are in the streets and how few women.

I have heard in Spain that the women of Seville are very pretty, but if I am to tell the truth and judge from the ones in the streets, they don't appeal to me. I have seen in the North and in Madrid much better-looking women, with the same Southern characteristics.

Indeed, in Spain there is no great difference between the people of the North and those of the South; not like in Italy; here, as far as I can see, one can hardly tell an Andalusian from a Basque and a Galician from a Catalan.

From the window of the café I watch, feeling a little tired, the crowds of men that fill the street. Many of them must be bullfighters because they wear a braid like the Chinese, a small braid turned upwards that looks like a pig's tail.

Among these anemic, blurred, expressionless faces, there are some tall, energetic, looking men, who remind me of the Roman sculptures in the Museum in Florence. Many others are leaning against the wall in an attitude of listlessness and indolence. "Are you tired or shall we go for another walk?" Juan asked me. "No, let's go."

We leave the café. It's nearly ten o'clock and many stores are still open. The continuous coming and going of people goes on.

Key to exercises and drills

CHAPTER 1

Exercise 1: 1 los libros. 2 las casas. 3 las mujeres. 4 los hombres. 5 las calles. 6 las flores. 7 los jardines. 8 los coches. 9 las capitales. 10 las ciudades. 11 las luces. 12 las leyes.

Exercise 2: 1 los. 2 el. 3 las. 4 la. 5 el. 6 los. 7 el. 8 la. 9 el. 10 las. 11 el. 12 el.

Exercise 2 (indefinite articles): 1 unos; 2 un; 3 unas; 4 una; 5 un; 6 unos; 7 un; 8 una; 9 un; 10 unas; 11 un; 12 un.

Exercise 3: 1 el libro. 2 la mesa. 3 los billetes. 4 unos árboles. 5 una cerveza. 6 el coche. 7 una ciudad. 8 unos cigarrillos. 9 el jardín. 10 una calle. 11 unas mujeres. 12 la estación.

Exercise 4: 1 tienen una casa. 2 no tenemos café. 3 el hombre tiene miedo. 4 tengo que trabajar. 5 ¿tienes un lápiz? 6 no tienen sed. 7 ¿tienen Vds. todo? 8 tengo calor. 9 tenemos que salir. 10 tiene un hijo.

Drill 1: 1 no, no tengo hambre. 2 no, no tenemos cerveza. 3 no, no tengo sed. 4 no, no tenemos calor. 5 no, no tengo frío. 6 no, no tenemos los libros. 7 no, no tengo cigarrillos. 8 no, no tenemos los billetes.

CHAPTER 2

Exercise 5: 1 a la iglesia. 2 del idioma. 3 al coche. 4 a la mesa. 5 de los árboles. 6 a la casa. 7 del hombre. 8 de la ciudad. 9 a la calle. 10 del vino. 11 al policía. 12 de la estación.

Exercise 6: 1 buenos. 2 encantadora. 3 útiles. 4 blancas. 5 barato. 6 larga. 7 altos. 8 interesantes. 9 inglés. 10 alemana.

Exercise 7: 1 son. 2 está. 3 son. 4 es. 5 están. 6 está. 7 es. 8 es. 9 está. 10 estoy.

Exercise 8: 1 es italiana. 2 las manzanas están en la cocina.
3 el autobús está allí. 4 Madrid es la capital de España.
5 la chica es alta. 6 la casa está en la colina. 7 es peligroso
fumar. 8 el café está demasiado dulce. 9 mañana es domingo.
10 están en la playa.

CHAPTER 3

Exercise 9: 1 ese coche es caro. 2 esos cigarrillos son fuertes.
3 esa iglesia es muy vieja. 4 estos amigos son de Málaga. 5 esta
mesa está ocupada. 6 ese hombre está libre. 7 este ascensor está
lleno. 8 esas uvas están agrias. 9 aquellos libros son
interesantes. 10 es aquella playa.

Exercise 10: 1 estos, ésos. 2 esa, aquélla. 3 estas, ésas. 4 ese,
éste. 5 este, aquél. 6 esos, éstos. 7 este, ése. 8 ese, éste. 9 estas,
ésas. 10 este, aquél.

Exercise 11: 1 compro. 2 fuma. 3 Vd. bebe. 4 escribimos.
5 aprenden. 6 estudio. 7 hablas. 8 come. 9 vivimos. 10 suben.
11 aprendo. 12 bebe.

Exercise 12: 1 compra un periódico. 2 ¿bebe cerveza? 3 Pedro
vive en Barcelona. 4 escribo a Conchita. 5 ¿estudias inglés?
6 estos niños aprenden español. 7 come demasiado. 8 subimos
la colina. 9 hablo inglés. 10 fuman cigarrillos baratos.

Exercise 13: 1 el pueblo en el que vivimos. 2 la mujer que
trabaja en la tienda. 3 el libro que tengo que leer. 4 la ciudad
de la que estamos hablando. 5 es Pedro quien es médico.
6 ¿de quién son estas cartas? 7 ¿qué revista está comprando?
8 la casa que tiene una puerta verde. 9 la pluma con la que
escribo. 10 ¿cuál es el número?

Drill 2: 1 sí, bebemos cerveza. 2 sí, como pan. 3 sí, vivimos en
Boston. 4 sí, soy médico. 5 sí, hablamos español. 6 sí, compro
la revista.

Drill 3: 1 no, no vivo en Barcelona. 2 no, no fumamos.
3 no, no aprendo alemán. 4 no, no compramos los periódicos.
5 no, no bebo vino. 6 no, no somos españoles.

Drill 4: 1 está comprando. 2 están bebiendo. 3 estoy
estudiando. 4 estamos comiendo. 5 está leyendo. 6 estoy
fumando. 7 estamos hablando. 8 está escribiendo. 9 están
aprendiendo. 10 estoy subiendo.

CHAPTER 4

Exercise 14: 1 mi marido. 2 su hermano. 3 nuestra hermana.
4 su sobrino. 5 su tío. 6 mis padres. 7 tu mujer. 8 sus hijos.
9 su primo. 10 sus parientes.

Exercise 15: 1 la tuya. 2 el suyo. 3 el nuestro. 4 la suya.
5 la nuestra. 6 el mío. 7 la suya. 8 los vuestros. 9 la mía.
10 el suyo.

Exercise 16: 1 diez casas. 2 setenta y dos pesetas. 3 doscientos
cigarrillos. 4 dieciséis cartas. 5 ciento treinta y cinco libros.
6 cuarenta y seis hoteles. 7 trescientas cincuenta y cuatro
manzanas. 8 sesenta y ocho tiendas. 9 mil cuatrocientos
hombres. 10 setecientos ochenta y cinco coches.

Exercise 17: 1 el séptimo libro. 2 la primera mujer. 3 la tercera
hija. 4 el sexto cigarrillo. 5 la segunda puerta. 6 el décimo día.
7 la cuarta calle. 8 el noveno niño. 9 el quinto hombre.
10 la octava tienda.

Exercise 18: 1 ¿qué hora es? 2 son las diez y veinte en mi
reloj. 3 trabajo hasta las once y media. 4 el invierno en Madrid
es frío. 5 tienen sus vacaciones en julio. 6 mi cumpleaños es el
tres de enero. 7 está libre los sábados. 8 octubre es
generalmente un mes bonito. 9 tenemos que ir a Barcelona
en mayo. 10 los domingos ceno con mis padres.

REVISION – 1

Exercise 1: 1 tengo. 2 viven. 3 es. 4 están. 5 comen. 6 habla.
7 son. 8 cena. 9 aprende. 10 trabajamos.

Exercise 2: 1 en España los periódicos americanos son muy
caros. 2 ¿dónde están las maletas? 3 la habitación está en el
tercer piso. 4 en el verano viven en Estados Unidos y en el
invierno viven en España. 5 su marido está enfermo, bebe
demasiado. 6 tengo que escribir a mi amiga alemana. 7 estas
flores son para la madre de Juan. 8 la Sra. Suárez es una mujer
encantadora. 9 tenemos que comprar los billetes. 10 ¿qué hora
es? son las siete y cuarto. 11 ¿es ese perro suyo? 12 nuestra hija
está aprendiendo español.

Exercise 3: 1 soy americano(a). 2 no, vivo en Delaware. 3 estoy
de vacaciones. 4 sólo dos. 5 sí, trabajo en una tienda. 6 es una
librería. 7 no, estoy en casa de una amiga. 8 en una casa en la
playa. 9 no, gracias, tengo prisa. Adiós.

CHAPTER 5

Exercise 19: 1 vamos a la iglesia los domingos. 2 voy a comprar ese libro. 3 va a casa de su amigo. 4 vamos de vacaciones en el verano. 5 van a Madrid en tren. 6 vamos a tomar un café. 7 no va a cantar. 8 mañana voy a descansar. 9 van de compras en el mercado. 10 vamos al teatro.

Exercise 20: 1 he escrito tres cartas. 2 han hablado en español. 3 hemos comido demasiado. 4 hay azúcar en este té. 5 ha comprado un vestido nuevo. 6 ¿has terminado el trabajo? 7 nunca ha ayudado en la casa. 8 hay unas naranjas en la bolsa. 9 ¿ha bebido Vd. la cerveza? 10 no he visto la película.

Exercise 21: 1 a. 2 a. 3 –. 4 al. 5 –. 6 a. 7 –. 8 –. 9 –. 10 a.

Exercise 22: 1 visita a su madre. 2 he visto a la mujer. 3 tenemos que llamar a los niños. 4 María prepara la comida. 5 han invitado a sus amigos. 6 tiene una hermana casada. 7 voy a comprar un caballo. 8 tenemos que bañar al perro. 9 están esperando al profesor. 10 Carlos no ha visto Toledo.

Exercise 23: 1 Juan se lo ofrece; 2 la bebo por la mañana; 3 lo hemos comprado; 4 me las ha enviado; 5 se la he escrito; 6 los comemos; 7 estos señores no lo comprenden; 8 tengo que estudiarla; 9 nos las ha vendido; 10 se los hemos dado.

Exercise 24: 1 no fume Vd. esos cigarrillos. 2 beba Vd. este vino. 3 envíeme Vd. la revista. 4 léales Vd. la carta. 5 véndale Vd. su reloj. 6 aprenda Vd. estos números. 7 escriba Vd. su nombre aquí. 8 no coma Vd. esas manzanas. 9 no compre Vd. esa carne. 10 no me los dé Vd.

Exercise 24 (plurals): 1 no fumen Vds. 2 beban Vds. 3 envíenme Vds. 4 léanles Vds. 5 véndanle Vds. 6 aprendan Vds. 7 escriban Vds. 8 no coman Vds. 9 no compren Vds. 10 no me los den Vds.

Drill 5: 1 no, voy a tomarla ahora. 2 no, van a ir ahora. 3 no, va a escribirla ahora. 4 no, vamos a hacerlo ahora. 5 no, voy a comprarlos ahora. 6 no, van a verle ahora. 7 no, vamos a terminarla ahora. 8 no, va a llamarla ahora. 9 no, voy a subirlas ahora. 10 no, vamos a beberlo ahora.

Drill 6: 1 sí, cómprelo. 2 sí, súbanlas. 3 sí, llámele. 4 sí, invítenles. 5 sí, léala. 6 sí, envíenlas. 7 sí, bébala. 8 sí, véndanla.

Drill 7: 1 ya lo he preparado. 2 ya le hemos llamado. 3 ya lo he escrito. 4 ya la hemos tomado. 5 ya los he comprado. 6 ya les hemos hablado. 7 ya los he contado. 8 ya lo hemos vendido. 9 ya la he leído.

CHAPTER 6

Exercise 25: 1 Pedro y Anita se escriben todos los días. 2 el coche va a pararse. 3 vamos a casarnos. 4 los niños se acuestan a las ocho. 5 tenemos que lavarnos. 6 los dos hombres se odian. 7 siempre me pide dinero. 8 nunca se ayudan. 9 Carlos vuelve de la oficina a las seis y media. 10 tengo que dormirme. 11 llévese Vd. estas tazas. 12 la calle se llama Baeza. 13 voy a sentarme aquí. 14 nos vamos mañana. 15 me he decidido a vivir en España.

Exercise 26: 1 estamos trabajando con ellos. 2 ha comprado un regalo para mí. 3 ¿va a volver con Vd.? 4 el tiempo está contra nosotros. 5 se han ido sin él. 6 siempre ha vivido conmigo. 7 estas cartas son para ella. 8 van a comprar la casa entre ellos. 9 ¿están los niños contigo? 10 según él, el viaje es demasiado largo.

Exercise 27: 1 ¿qué tiempo hace? 2 hoy hace mucho frío. 3 va a llover mañana. 4 no me gusta esta cerveza. 5 va a traernos café. 6 le gusta salir todas las tardes. 7 no sé dónde está. 8 van a España porque les gusta el sol. 9 hace veinticinco años. 10 a Carmen le gusta sentarse en el jardín.

Drill 8: 1 sí, me gusta mucho. 2 sí, le gustan mucho. 3 sí, nos gusta mucho. 4 sí, nos gusta mucho. 5 sí, le gusta mucho. 6 sí, me gustan mucho. 7 sí, me gusta mucho. 8 sí, les gusta mucho. 9 sí, nos gusta mucho. 10 sí, les gusta mucho.

Drill 9: 1 sí, trabajo con ella. 2 sí, es para Vds. 3 sí, vuelve conmigo. 4 sí, vamos sin ellos. 5 sí, son para Vd. 6 sí, vive con ellos. 7 sí, son para nosotros. 8 sí, voy sin él.

Drill 10: 1 sí, quisiera sentarme. 2 sí, quisiera lavarme. 3 sí, quisiera dormirme. 4 sí, quisiera irme. 5 sí, quisiera pararme. 6 sí, quisiéramos sentarnos. 7 sí, quisiéramos lavarnos. 8 sí, quisiéramos dormirnos. 9 sí, quisiéramos irnos. 10 sí, quisiéramos pararnos.

CHAPTER 7

Exercise 28: 1 Luis fumaba un cigarrillo. 2 generalmente la veo por la mañana. 3 habían hablado con el gerente del hotel. 4 solía traerme bombones. 5 el muchacho buscaba su maleta. 6 la representación solía empezar a las diez. 7 había trabajado en una fábrica. 8 el mar estaba muy frío. 9 la mujer nos miraba. 10 solíamos comer mucho pescado.

Exercise 29: 1 nada. 2 nadie. 3 ni, ni. 4 nunca. 5 ningún. 6 tampoco. 7 nadie. 8 nada. 9 ninguna. 10 nunca.

Exercise 30: 1 felizmente. 2 verdaderamente. 3 tristemente. 4 lentamente. 5 nuevamente. 6 agradablemente. 7 malamente. 8 ciertamente. 9 rápidamente. 10 claramente.

Exercise 31: 1 mi hermano es más fuerte que yo. 2 este jerez es más seco que ése. 3 Carlos es tres años mayor que María. 4 los zapatos negros son más pequeños que los azules. 5 su coche es mejor que el mío. 6 escribe peor que su hermana. 7 he llegado más pronto que mi padre. 8 no tienen tanto dinero como sus amigos. 9 no necesito tantas maletas como tú. 10 el agua en la piscina está más caliente que en el mar.

Drill 11: 1 sí, solía verla. 2 sí, solían comer. 3 sí, solíamos trabajar. 4 sí, solía escribirlas. 5 sí, solía viajar. 6 sí, solíamos ir. 7 sí, solía hablarlo. 8 sí, solía invitarles. 9 sí, solían tenerlo. 10 sí, solía beberlo.

Drill 12: 1 no, no quiero nada. 2 no, no han vivido aquí nunca. 3 no, no queremos ni té ni café. 4 no, no hay ningún turista inglés. 5 no, no conocemos a nadie. 6 no, no tengo ninguna revista española.

Drill 13: 1 los míos son más viejos. 2 el mío es peor. 3 el mío es más bonito. 4 el mío es mejor. 5 el mío es más alto. 6 los míos son más caros. 7 las mías son más grandes. 8 los míos son más baratos.

REVISION – 2

Drill 1: 1 nos gusta más el vino. 2 nos gusta más la carne. 3 le gusta más la playa. 3 me gusta más el rugby. 5 les gusta más jugar. 6 me gusta más Barcelona.

Exercise 1: 1 voy a una fiesta mañana y necesito un vestido nuevo. 2 hemos visto una película muy buena en el 'Roxy'. 3 no puede venir a la playa con nosotros, tiene demasiado trabajo. 4 Pedro es muy simpático, pero no tiene paciencia con los niños. 5 la representación no empieza hasta las diez y cuarto - es demasiado tarde para nosotros. 6 no han podido salir porque ha llovido todo el día. 7 tenemos que esperar hasta las cuatro y media porque las tiendas están cerradas. 8 los ingleses beben más jerez que los españoles.

Drill 2: 1 sí, lávelo. 2 no, no la espere. 3 sí, pregúntele. 4 no, no se las lleve. 5 sí, llámele. 6 no, no le invite. 7 sí, póngalas. 8 no, no lo haga.

Drill 3: 1 sí, termínenlo. 2 no, no lo pidan. 3 sí, véanla. 4 no, no se bañen. 5 sí, cómprenlos. 6 no, no la preparen. 7 sí, envíenlas. 8 sí, ayúdenle.

Exercise 2: 1 (d). 2 (g). 3 (f). 4 (h). 5 (c). 6 (a). 7 (e). 8 (b).

Exercise 3: • Pasado mañana es el cumpleaños de Luisa. •¿Qué podemos comprarle? • Solo puedo pensar en bombones, flores . . . • Lee mucho y le gusta viajar. • ¿Por qué no le compramos un libro de viajes? • Entonces, vamos de compras esta tarde y buscamos algo.

CHAPTER 8

Exercise 32: 1 hemos tenido un buen viaje. 2 cada hombre tenía un trabajo. 3 es un gran pintor. 4 siempre llevan la misma ropa. 5 hay bastantes hoteles en esta zona. 6 la pobre mujer ha perdido su bolso. 7 tengo un sombrero nuevo. 8 hemos pedido otra bebida. 9 estos sellos son muy viejos. 10 todos los niños son buenos nadadores.

Exercise 33: 1 se casarán el próximo mes. 2 me acostaré temprano esta noche. 3 vendrá con nosotros de vacaciones. 4 les visitaremos el domingo. 5 no quieren hablar con nosotros. 6 sería mejor parar. 7 no me gustaría conducir un coche grande. 8 no tendrá que andar muy lejos. 9 no valdrían nada. 10 no podremos ver el museo. 11 no quería vender la casa. 12 el autocar saldrá a las ocho.

Exercise 34: 1 cierre Vd. las ventanas antes de acostarse. 2 tendré que pensar antes de decidir. 3 no puedes irte antes de

terminar el trabajo. 4 ha pasado el día sin hablar con nadie.
5 lloraba sin saber por qué. 6 se sentían enfermos después de
comer marisco. 7 tenía mucho sueño después de trabajar toda
la noche. 8 nos gustaría ver la habitación antes de tomarla.
9 su voz estaba ronca de gritar tanto. 10 después de escribir la
carta enséñemela Vd.

Drill 14: 1 no, le verán luego. 2 no, lo terminaremos luego.
3 no, iré luego. 4 no, la escribirá luego. 5 no, las enviaremos
luego. 6 no, la cerrarán luego. 7 no, saldrá luego. 8 no, la haré
luego. 9 no, las verán luego. 10 no, las abriré luego.

Drill 15: 1 hace seis meses que estudio español. 2 hace tres
años que estamos en Madrid. 3 hace dos semanas que trabajan
aquí. 4 hace un año que vive en Detroit. 5 hace diez minutos
que espero. 6 llevo seis meses estudiando español.
7 llevamos tres años en Madrid. 8 llevan dos semanas
trabajando aquí. 9 lleva un año viviendo en Detroit.
10 llevo diez minutos esperando.

CHAPTER 9

Exercise 35: 1 dimos un paseo por el río. 2 no quisieron
verme. 3 puse la carta en el sobre. 4 murió dos años después.
5 pagó la comida con un cheque. 6 el camarero nos trajo las
bebidas y se fue. 7 anduvieron cinco kilómetros buscando un
garaje. 8 salí a las diez y volví a la hora de comer. 9 le dijimos
que su padre había llegado. 10 no hizo nada toda la mañana.

Exercise 36: 1 salió. 2 estaba, sonó. 3 viajaban, tuvieron.
4 jugaban, empezó. 5 bajó, hacía. 6 se sentaba. 7 volví. 8 hacía,
llegamos. 9 recibió, vivía. 10 preguntó.

Exercise 37: 1 no conocen ese disco. 2 sabe que quiero un
ordenador. 3 ese programa de televisión es divertidísimo.
4 esta talla es la más pequeña que tenemos. 5 estos zapatos son
los más bonitos, ésos son los más baratos. 6 es el hombre más
amable que conozco. 7 no saben que deseo verles. 8 fue una
conversación interesantísima. 9 es la iglesia más vieja de
esta ciudad. 10 la farmacia estaba lejísimos de la parada de
autobús.

Exercise 38: 1 el té es una bebida muy agradable. 2 la señora
Collado llegará el domingo. 3 se puso los guantes porque hacía

frío. 4 él es camarero y ella es dependienta. 5 pasé dos semanas en el hospital. 6 lo importante es no preocuparse. 7 la pobre María se ha roto el brazo derecho. 8 los libros son muy caros hoy día. 9 andaba con gran dificultad. 10 va a traer otra taza. 11 bebimos media botella de coñac. 12 lo mejor es vender la casa.

Drill 16: 1 pero tuvo que escribirla. 2 pero tuvieron que pagarla. 3 pero tuve que verle. 4 pero tuvimos que ir. 5 pero tuvo que salir. 6 pero tuvo que hacerla. 7 pero tuvo que comerlo. 8 pero tuvo que fumarlo. 9 pero tuve que dárselo. 10 pero tuvimos que beberla.

Drill 17: 1 no, estuvimos ayer. 2 no, vinieron ayer. 3 no, lo compré ayer. 4 no, la pagaron ayer. 5 no, la recibió ayer. 6 no, las hicimos ayer. 7 no, llovió ayer. 8 no, las trajeron ayer. 9 no, fuimos ayer. 10 no, les visité ayer.

Drill 18: 1 sí, es el más bonito que he visto. 2 sí, son los más caros que he visto. 3 sí, es la más grande que he visto. 4 sí, es el más elegante que he visto. 5 sí, son los más divertidos que he visto. 6 sí, son las más pequeñas que he visto.

CHAPTER 10

Exercise 39: 1 por. 2 por. 3 para. 4 por. 5 para. 6 para. 7 por. 8 para. 9 para. 10 por.

Exercise 40: 1 tenemos que pasar por la Aduana. 2 nos cobraron dos mil pesetas por la comida. 3 es demasiado tarde para ir al cine. 4 necesito una bolsa para todas mis compras. 5 ¿tiene Vd. una llave para abrir este armario? 6 este libro es demasiado difícil para él. 7 el avión sale para Madrid a las siete y cuarto. 8 haría cualquier cosa por él. 9 leímos la carta por curiosidad. 10 quiere comprar unos melocotones para su madre.

Exercise 41: 1 la casa fue construida por su abuelo. 2 fui acusado del robo. 3 el barco se vendió por ochenta mil pesetas. 4 el trabajo está terminado ahora. 5 se cree que está muerto. 6 las montañas estaban cubiertas de nieve. 7 la cena no se sirve hasta las nueve. 8 las ventanas se pintaron hace tres semanas. 9 fueron recibidos por uno de los directores. 10 el programa fue presentado por un famoso actor.

Exercise 42: 1 jugué con los niños toda la tarde. 2 están construyendo un aparcamiento nuevo. 3 oyó un ruido arriba. 4 me sequé los pies al fuego. 5 cayeron al suelo. 6 está leyendo las instrucciones. 7 huyeron de España al principio de la guerra. 8 pagué mucho dinero por ese cuadro. 9 coja Vd. el equipaje, por favor. 10 creyó que la tienda estaba cerrada.

Exercise 43: 1 conseguí hablar con ellos. 2 nos aconsejó alquilar un coche. 3 trataron de entrar en la habitación. 4 pienso quejarme del servicio. 5 estamos aprendiendo a jugar al tenis. 6 volví a llamarle. 7 el señor Solís acaba de llegar. 8 se cansó de subir y se sentó. 9 dejó de llover y salió el sol. 10 me olvidé de darle el recado. 11 insistieron en pagar sus billetes. 12 el paquete tardó dos semanas en llegar. 13 acabaron por tener una discusión. 14 la mujer se esforzó por sonreír. 15 el hombre amenazó con llamar a la policía. 16 se contenta con ganar muy poco.

Drill 19: 1 para. 2 por. 3 para. 4 para. 5 por. 6 para. 7 para. 8 por.

Drill 20: 1 el libro se publicó. 2 los coches se alquilaron. 3 la puerta se abrió. 4 los ruidos se oyeron. 5 el trabajo se terminó. 6 la casa se construyó. 7 los barcos se vendieron. 8 la carta se leyó.

Drill 21: 1 sí, acabo de comprarlos. 2 sí, acaban de llegar. 3 sí, acabo de recibirlas. 4 sí, acabamos de hacerlas. 5 sí, acaban de acostarse. 6 sí, acabo de encontrarla.

REVISION – 3

Exercise 1: 1 iremos. 2 cuidará. 3 trabajaré. 4 se levantará. 5 saldremos. 6 vendrá. 7 hará. 8 diré. 9 podrán. 10 tendrás.

Exercise 2: 1 traería. 2 volverían. 3 viajaría. 4 pagarían. 5 enviaría. 6 tendrían.

Exercise 3: 1 anoche vi a Antonio con su mujer. 2 el tren llegó dos horas tarde. 3 ofreció ayudarme con las bolsas. 4 no necesitamos ninguna ropa de invierno. 5 vendieron la casa a un amigo suyo. 6 conduje cien kilómetros sin parar. 7 fue a buscar una farmacia. 8 no le gustó el libro que le di.

Exercise 4: • Muy bien. Fue un viaje muy interesante.
• Fuimos a Córdoba, Granada y Sevilla. • Mi mujer había
estado en Sevilla, pero yo no conocía ninguna de ellas.
• No sé. Es difícil elegir una. Cada una tiene una belleza
diferente. Posiblemente Granada. La Alhambra es
maravillosa. • Alberto, me gustaría seguir hablando, pero
tengo que ir de compras con mi mujer. Estará esperándome.
Te llamaré el viernes.

Exercise 5: 1 ¿por qué necesitas dinero? 2 lo necesito para
comprar un coche nuevo. 3 salieron ayer para Venezuela.
4 estoy haciendo esto por ti. 5 estamos demasiado cansados
para andar a la estación. 6 el hotel cuesta ocho mil pesetas
por persona. 7 me ha invitado a su casa por un mes. 8 me
enviaron una postal para decirme que venían.

Exercise 6: 1 se han cancelado los vuelos. 2 le acompañó su
mujer. 3 se ha censurado la película. 4 se anunciaron las
elecciones en octubre. 5 la policía arrestó al muchacho.
6 el Rey inauguró la exposición. 7 la explosión se oyó en todo
el pueblo. 8 el banco no ha aceptado el cheque.

Exercise 7: 1 de, a. 2 a. 3 –. 4 a, de. 5 en. 6 a. 7 a. 8 –. 9 –.
10 de. 11 en. 12 –. 13 a. 14 –. 15 de. 16 con.

Exercise 8: 1 todos estamos cansados hoy. 2 mi hijo quiere ser
abogado. 3 cuando estuvo enfermo, yo iba a visitarle todos los
días. 4 no te sientes en esa silla, está rota. 5 hace mucho calor,
aunque todas las ventanas están abiertas. 6 está triste porque
su mejor amigo se ha muerto. 7 siempre estoy en casa los
domingos. 8 es una mujer muy inteligente, pero no muy
amable. 9 ¿quién es usted? soy un amigo suyo. 10 estábamos
para salir cuando él llegó. 11 no le dieron el trabajo porque era
demasiado joven. 12 éstas no son mis maletas, las mías son
negras.

Exercise 9: 1 íbamos, nos quedábamos. 2 hizo, pidió. 3 tenía,
podía. 4 llamó, estaba. 5 llevábamos, llegó. 6 fueron, volvieron,
hacía. 7 llegué, estaba. 8 dejó, di. 9 salió, había. 10 trabajó,
estaba.

CHAPTER 11

Exercise 44: 1 ¿cuánto le debo? 2 no deberían decir esas
cosas. 3 debe de tener un buen trabajo. 4 debo ver a un médico.
5 ¿sabe hablar español? 6 no puedo leer sin gafas.
7 deberíamos ir allí más a menudo. 8 me debe una explicación.
9 esa sortija debe de costar mucho dinero. 10 no sé montar en
bicicleta. 11 no puede dormir sin tomar píldoras. 12 ¿sabe Vd.
guisar?

Exercise 45: 1 me alegro de que puedan venir. 2 quiere que el
abogado vea los documentos. 3 nos han mandado que
esperemos aquí. 4 dudo que salga el sol. 5 me sorprende que
no haya escrito. 6 me ha pedido que le enseñe español.
7 es posible que se hayan perdido. 8 es una lástima que no
tengamos bastante dinero. 9 es probable que se casen.
10 no podré hacerlo a no ser que me ayuden. 11 iremos al cine
con tal que me dejes pagar. 12 esperará hasta que yo vuelva.
13 tendrán que comerlo, aunque no les guste. 14 no hay nadie
que pueda pagar ese precio. 15 ¿hay alguien que sepa tocar el
piano? 16 necesito una mujer que cuide de los niños.
17 lo encontraremos, dondequiera que esté. 18 te ayudará
cuandoquiera que tengas un problema. 19 por mucho que
trate, nunca tendrá éxito. 20 por muy fácil que parezca, se
necesita práctica.

Exercise 46: 1 hazlo, no lo hagas. 2 ven, no vengas. 3 acuéstate,
no te acuestes. 4 aprende, no aprendas. 5 ponlo, no lo pongas. 6
escríbela, no la escribas. 7 grita, no grites. 8 óyelo, no lo oigas.
9 preocúpate, no te preocupes. 10 duérmete, no te duermas.

Exercise 47: 1 no te enfades. 2 escuchadme. 3 vístete.
4 no me digáis eso. 5 tened cuidado. 6 léenoslo. 7 callaos.
8 no me despiertes temprano. 9 perdonad mi error.
10 no muevas el coche.

Drill 22: 1 sí, debe de estar enfermo. 2 sí, deben de ser las
cinco. 3 sí, deben de estar muy tristes. 4 sí, debe de trabajar
mucho. 5 sí, debe de hacer muchos años. 6 sí, deben de estar
en casa.

Drill 23: 1 sí, es preferible que coman. 2 sí, es preferible que se vaya. 3 sí, es preferible que volvamos. 4 sí, es preferible que se acuesten. 5 sí, es preferible que pague. 6 sí, es preferible que nos sentemos.

Drill 24: 1 sí, pedidlos. 2 sí, tráelo. 3 sí, llamadle. 4 sí, cómpralo. 5 sí, abridlas. 6 sí, ayúdale.

Drill 25: 1 no, siguen comiendo. 2 no, sigue leyéndolo. 3 no, seguimos trabajando. 4 no, sigo pintando. 5 no, sigue cantando. 6 no, siguen construyéndola.

CHAPTER 12

Exercise 48: 1 querían que viajase con ellos. 2 tenía miedo de que hubiera tenido un accidente. 3 nos dijo que pusiéramos la mesa. 4 le pedí que se diera prisa. 5 esperábamos que no hiciese demasiado calor en Sevilla. 6 dondequiera que fuese, siempre encontraba amigos. 7 le avisé que no usara esa máquina. 8 me llamó por teléfono para que reservara las habitaciones. 9 buscaban a una persona que pudiese traducir la carta. 10 me alegro de que ganaran el primer premio.

Exercise 49: 1 lo haría si pudiera. 2 si hace buen tiempo, trabajaré en el jardín. 3 el perro no te habría mordido si no le hubieses pegado. 4 si les preguntaras, no sabrían que decir. 5 si le viera ahora, no le hablaría. 6 Vd. no habría perdido el dinero, si lo hubiera guardado en su bolsillo. 7 si vinieran a la fiesta, se divertirían. 8 te escribiré, si tengo que quedarme allí más tiempo. 9 si no llevas un paraguas, te mojarás. 10 yo iría al concierto, si él viniera conmigo.

Exercise 50: 1 ojalá no tuviera que trabajar. 2 quizá esté enfermo. 3 puede que haya perdido el tren. 4 que venga, si quiere. 5 ojalá pudiéramos tener unas vacaciones. 6 pase lo que pase, estaré en contacto con Vd. 7 ¿podemos ver las fotografías? 8 dijo que yo podía tener el día libre. 9 ¡que se divierta Vd! 10 quizá no vieran el aviso.

Exercise 51: 1 no te acerques al borde. 2 se asomó a la ventanilla del coche. 3 mi hermano va a casarse con una chica inglesa; 4 sabes que puedes contar conmigo. 5 la ventana daba a una calle muy concurrida. 6 el éxito de la obra depende de los actores. 7 tengo que despedirme de mis compañeros.

8 no dudan de su buena intención. 9 María se ha enamorado de un hombre muy tonto. 10 es muy fácil encontrarse con turistas ingleses en España. 11 no hemos podido enterarnos de su nombre. 12 no me fijé en lo que llevaba. 13 tienes que ocuparte de las bebidas. 14 esta casa se parece mucho a la nuestra. 15 no quiere pensar en todos los problemas. 16 no sabemos lo que piensa de la situación. 17 este helado sabe a fresa. 18 soñaba con todos los lugares que había visitado.

Drill 26: 1 puede que lo venda. 2 puede que se casen. 3 puede que salgamos. 4 puede que vuelva. 5 puede que nos inviten. 6 puede que nade.

Drill 27: 1 vendrían si pudieran. 2 lo pediríamos si lo necesitáramos. 3 comería si tuviera hambre. 4 se lo diríamos si le viéramos. 5 saldrían si no lloviera. 6 te lo daría si lo encontrara. 7 trabajaría más si le pagaran bien. 8 hablaría con ellos si vinieran.

Drill 28: 1 se sorprendió al oír la noticia. 2 gritaron al ver a los policías. 3 lloraba al leer la carta. 4 me pidió la llave al salir. 5 tuve miedo al oír un ruido. 6 se lavaron las manos al terminar. 7 me quité el sombrero al entrar. 8 empezó a llover al llegar a casa.

CHAPTER 13

Exercise 52: 1 mucha gente asistió al entierro. 2 esta cantidad de harina bastará. 3 esa caja no cabe en el maletero. 4 quiero devolver la revista que me prestó. 5 echó la pelota a los niños. 6 voy a echar el vino. 7 les falta experiencia. 8 faltan cinco libros de este estante. 9 nos hacen falta más ayudantes. 10 meterán toda la ropa en una maleta. 11 ¿cuántos días te quedan? 12 quitará estas sillas. 13 ¿puedo quitarme la chaqueta? 14 sobran huevos para hacer la tortilla. 15 es muy agradable tocar seda. 16 le gustaría tocar el violín. 17 tomó la pluma y firmó la carta. 18 les gusta tomar vino con su comida.

Exercise 53: 1 ha heredado más de veinte millones de pesetas. 2 no puedo venderlo por menos de diez mil pesetas. 3 hemos vivido en Madrid más de quince años. 4 lo haré en menos de cinco minutos. 5 nunca había visto un collar tan bonito. 6 ¡qué edificio tan feo! 7 no haría tal cosa.

8 encuentro tales libros muy aburridos. 9 ese no es mi hermano, sino mi primo. 10 no tienen un perro, pero tienen dos gatos. 11 tiene más dinero de lo que dice. 12 son más listos de lo que crees. 13 ¡qué idea tan buena! 14 ¡es un viaje tan largo!

Exercise 54: 1 el hombre dormía bajo un árbol. 2 me escribió desde Córdoba. 3 después del teatro, fuimos a su casa. 4 es muy espléndido con sus amigos. 5 esperamos a la puerta, pero no vino. 6 según su padre, está muy enfermo. 7 había un fila larga de coches delante de mí. 8 tuvo que presentarse ante el juez. 9 se fueron sin pagar la bebida. 10 puso la maleta debajo de la cama. 11 hay una zapatería enfrente de la panadería. 12 no te veré hasta el domingo. 13 el ascensor se paró entre los dos pisos. 14 quiero probarlo antes de comprarlo. 15 empezaremos a andar hacia la estación. 16 tendrán que ir en el autobús. 17 el libro ha caído detrás del sofá. 18 dejaré el paquete encima del escritorio.

Drill 29: 1 no, no le hace falta. 2 no, no nos hace falta. 3 no, no me hacen falta. 4 no, no les hace falta. 5 no, no le hacen falta. 6 no, no nos hace falta.

Drill 30: 1 no podemos devolverlo todavía. 2 no puedo meterla todavía. 3 no pueden echarlas todavía. 4 no puedo quitármelos todavía. 5 no podemos tomarlo todavía. 6 no puede pagarla todavía.

Drill 31: 1 hasta. 2 desde. 3 enfrente de. 4 encima de. 5 entre. 6 sin. 7 con. 8 antes de. 9 en. 10 hacia.

REVISION – 4

Exercise 1: 1 deben de haber salido. 2 no sabía ni leer, ni escribir. 3 deberíamos esperar unos minutos más. 4 ¿puede usted decirme la hora? 5 tenía miedo porque no sabía nadar. 6 deberías invitarla a cenar. 7 me deben dos mil pesetas. 8 debéis decidir lo que queréis hacer.

Exercise 2: 1 vayamos. 6 ayude. 3 se queden. 4 salga. 5 sepa. 6 pueda. 7 llueva. 8 tengáis. 9 juegue. 10 llegues. 11 veamos. 12 venga. 13 llame. 14 tengan. 15 haga. 16 acompañe.

Exercise 3: 1 espera. 2 siéntate. 3 dale. 4 haz. 5 pidas. 6 ten. 7 traigas. 8 ven.

Exercise 4: 1 limpiad. 2 volváis. 3 comed. 4 acostaos. 5 le digáis. 6 vayáis. 7 escribíd. 8 me telefoneéis.

Exercise 5: 1 estuviera / estuviese. 2 enviara / enviase. 3 perdonáramos / perdonásemos. 4 fuera / fuese. 5 supiéramos / supiésemos. 6 pudieras / pudieses. 7 firmaran / firmasen. 8 hiciera / hiciese. 9 fuera / fuese. 10 necesitaras / necesitases. 11 vendiéramos / vendiésemos. 12 trajera / trajese.

Exercise 6: • Ya lo sé. He tenido mucho trabajo. • Lo siento. No tengo ninguna noche libre esta semana. • ¿El sábado de la semana próxima? • Ven a mi casa a las ocho. Tomaremos un aperitivo y luego decidiremos adónde ir a cenar. • Quizás tengas razón. ¿Quieres que haga una reserva en un restaurante no lejos de donde vivo? • Adiós y gracias por llamar.

Exercise 7: 1 tengo calor. 2 tenía miedo. 3 tenía frío. 4 tenemos sed. 5 tenían sueño. 6 teníamos prisa. 7 tenía gracia. 8 no tenían hambre. 9 no tengo suerte.

Exercise 8: 1 ese abrigo no te cae muy bien. 2 ha caído enfermo y le han llevado al hospital. 3 decidimos dar un paseo corto. 4 ¡date prisa! el tren sale a las diez menos cuarto. 5 nunca me da los buenos días. 6 empezaron a subir la montaña, pero pronto se dieron por vencidos. 7 he venido a despedirme. 8 no podemos echar la culpa a nadie. 9 debes de echar de menos a Pedro, era un buen amigo tuyo. 10 ¿echó usted la llave a la maleta antes de salir de la habitación? 11 no quiero que me lleves la contraria. 12 nos llevamos muy bien, nunca discutimos. 13 más vale llevar el paraguas. es posible que llueva.

Exercise 9: 1 ¡cuánta gente! 2 el hombre que vimos ayer es su marido. 3 ¿de quién son estas revistas? 4 ¿qué asiento prefieres? 5 ¡qué película tan aburrida! 6 la mujer para quien trabaja es actriz. 7 ¡qué difícil es verle! 8 la habitación en la que dormimos daba al mar. 9 los que necesiten más información, pueden preguntar a esa señora. 10 tienes que enseñarme el regalo que te ha dado. 11 somos nosotros quienes tenemos que enviarlo. 12 no quiso ir, lo cual me sorprendió. 13 le pregunté quién había venido, pero no me lo dijo. 14 esa es la mujer cuya casa han comprado. 15 son amigos con quienes siempre estoy en contacto. 16 lo que no comprendemos es por qué no ha escrito.

Mini-dictionary

The translations given are those that are found in the course. A complete dictionary (which you ought to have) will list alternatives. In the Spanish–English section, a noun's gender is indicated by the article "el" or "la," and the masculine singular form of an adjective is followed by **(-a/-os/-as)** to show its other forms when a change is needed for feminine and plural. That a Spanish headword is a verb will be clear from "to" appearing in the English translation. Remember also that CH, LL, and Ñ are individual letters in Spanish; thus a word like "mañana" is found after "manzana."

Spanish–English

a at, to, in ...
el **abogado** lawyer
el **abrigo** coat
abril April
abrir to open
aburrido (-a/-os/-as) boring
el **abuelo** grandfather
acabar to finish
acaso perhaps
el **accidente** accident
aceptar to accept
acercarse to approach
acompañar to accompany
aconsejar to advise
acordarse (de) to remember
acostarse to go to bed
el **actor** actor
la **actriz** actress
acusar to accuse
adiós good-bye
adonde where to
la **Aduana** Customs
el **aeropuerto** airport
la **agencia de viajes** travel
    agent's

agosto August
agradable pleasant
agrio (-a/-os/-as) sour
el **agua** water
ahora now
ahorrar to save (money/time)
alegrarse to be glad
alemán (alemana/-es/-as)
    German
al fuego by the fire
algo something
alguien someone, somebody
alguno (-a/-os/-as) some, any
alquilar to rent
alto (-a/-os/-as) tall
el **alumno** pupil
allí there
amable kind
amanecer to dawn
amenazar to threaten
a menudo often
el **amigo** friend
andar to walk
anochecer to get dark
ante before

antes de before
anunciar to announce
el **año** year
el **aparcamiento** parking lot
el **aperitivo** aperitif, drink
aprender to learn
apresar to seize
aquel (-la/-los/-las) that/those
(over there)
el **armario** cupboard, wardrobe
el **árbol** tree
el **arquitecto** architect
arrancar to start (a car)
arrestar to arrest
arriba upstairs
el **ascensor** elevator
así (que) thus, so
el **asiento** seat
asistir to assist, to attend
asomarse to lean out
el **autobús** bus
el **autocar** motor coach
el **automóvil** car
el **avión** airplane
avisar to warn
el **aviso** warning (sign)
el **ayudante** helper
ayudar to help
ayudarse to help each other
el **azúcar** sugar
azul blue

bailar to dance
el **baile** dance, dancing
bajar to go down
bajo under
la **bala** bullet
el **banco** bank
bañar to bath
bañarse to bathe (oneself)
el **baño** bathroom
barato (-a/-os/-as) cheap
la **barca** rowboat
el **barco** boat, ship
bastante enough, fairly
bastar to suffice, to be enough

beber to drink
la **bebida** drink
la **bicicleta** bicycle
bien well
el **billete** ticket, bill (money)
el **bocadillo** sandwich
la **boda** wedding
la **bolsa** bag
el **bolsillo** pocket
el **bolso** pocketbook
blanco (-a/-os/-as) white
los **bombones** chocolates
bonito (-a/-os/-as) pretty
el **borde** edge
la **botella** bottle
el **brazo** arm
la **buena intención** goodwill
bueno (-a/-os/-as) good
buscar to look for

el **caballo** horse
caber to fit in
cada each
el **café** coffee
la **caja** box
el **cajón** drawer
caliente hot, warm
el **calor** heat
callarse to be quiet
la **calle** street
la **cama** bed
el **camarero** waiter
el **cambio** change
el **camino** way
el **camión** truck
la **camisa** shirt
el **camisón** nightgown
el **campo** country(side)
cancelar to cancel
cansado (-a/-os/-as) tired
cansarse to get tired
cantar to sing
la **cantidad** amount
la **capital** capital
la **carne** meat
la **carnicería** butcher's shop

caro (-a/-os/-as) expensive
la carretera road
la carta letter
la casa house, home
casado (-a/-os/-as) married
casarse to get married
casi almost
castigar to punish
la casualidad coincidence
la catedral cathedral
celebrar to celebrate
la cena dinner
cenar to have dinner
censurar to censor
cerca near
las cerillas matches
cerrar to close
la cerveza beer
ciego (-a/-os/-as) blind
cierto (-a/-os/-as) certain
el cigarrillo cigarette
el cine movie
la ciudad city, town
claro of course
el cliente client
el clima climate
cobrar to charge
el coche car
la cocina kitchen
el colegio school
la colina hill
el color color
el collar necklace
el comedor dining room
comer to eat
la comida meal, food, lunch
como how, as, like
el compañero colleague, companion
la compañía de seguros insurance company
comprar to buy
las compras purchases, shopping
comprender to understand
comprenderse to understand each other

con with
el concierto concert
concurrido busy, crowded
conducir to drive
conocer to know
conseguir to obtain, to manage
consentir to consent
conservador conservative
construir to build
el contable accountant, book-keeper
el contacto contact
contar to count
contentarse to content oneself
contento (-a/-os/-as) happy, pleased
contestar to answer
contra against
la conversación conversation
el coñac brandy
la corbata (neck)tie
correcto (-a/-os/-as) correct, right
el correo mail
la cosa thing
la costa coast
costar to cost
la costumbre custom, habit
creer to believe
el cuadro picture
cual which
cualquier cosa anything
cuando when
cuanto how much
el cuarto room, fourth, quarter
cubierto (-a/-os/-as) covered
la cuenta check
cuidar to look after
la culpa blame, fault
el cumpleaños birthday
la curiosidad curiosity

la chaqueta jacket
el cheque check (in a restaurant)
la chica girl

el **daño** damage, injury
dar to give
darse prisa to hurry
dar un paseo to go for a walk
de of, from
debajo (de) under, underneath
deber must, to owe
decidir to decide
decidirse a to decide
décimo (-a/-os/-as) tenth
decir to say
dejar(se) to let, to allow, to leave behind
delante (de) in front
delicioso (-a/-os/-as) lovely, delicious
demasiado too, too much
demasiado (-a/-os/-as) too much, too many
depender to depend
la **dependienta** salesperson
el **deporte** sport
derecho right
el **desastre** disaster
el **desayuno** breakfast
descansar to rest
describir to describe
desde from
desear to wish, to want
despacio slowly
el **despacho** office
despertar to waken
despertarse to wake up
despedir to dismiss
despedirse to say good-bye
después (de) after
detrás (de) behind
devolver to return, to give back
el **día** day
el **día libre** day off
diciembre December
difícil difficult
dificultad difficulty
diligentemente diligently
el **dinero** money
directamente straight

el **director** director
el **disco** record, disc
la **discusión** argument
discutir to argue
disparar to shoot
dispuesto ready
divertido amusing
divertirse to have a good time
el **documento** document
el **domingo** Sunday
dormir to sleep
dormirse to go to sleep
el **dormitorio** bedroom
la **ducha** shower
dudar to doubt
dudoso (-a/-os/-as) doubtful
dulce sweet
durante during
durar to last

echar to throw, to pour
el **edificio** building
el the
empezar to begin
el **empleado** employee
en in
enamorarse to fall in love
encantado (-a/-os/-as) delighted
encantador charming
encima (de) on top of
encontrar to find
encontrarse con to meet, to come across
enero January
enfadarse to get angry
enfermo (-a/-os/-as) sick (ill)
enfrente de opposite
enseñar to show, to teach
enterarse to find out
el **entierro** funeral
entonces then, in that case
entrar to come in
entre between
enviar to send
el **equipaje** luggage
el **error** error

escoger to choose
escribir to write
el **escritorio** desk
escuchar to listen
la **escuela** school
ese (-a/-os/-as) that, those
esforzarse to make an effort
España Spain
esperar to wait, to expect,
   to hope
espléndido generous
esta noche tonight
la **estación** station, season
el **estante** shelf
estar to be
estar en contacto con to be in
   touch with
este (-a/-os/-as) this, these
estudiar to study
el **estudiante** student
estupendo (-a/-os/-as) fine
estúpido (-a/-os/-as) stupid
el **éxito** success
la **explicación** explanation

la **fábrica** factory
fácil easy
fácilmente easily
faltar to lack, to be missing
famoso (-a/-os/-as) famous
farmacia drugstore
febrero February
la **fecha** date
feliz happy
feo (-a/-os/-as) ugly
la **fiesta** party
fijarse en to notice
la **fila** line, row
el **fin** end
firmar to sign
la **flor** flower
la **fotografía** photograph
francés (francesa/-es/-as)
   French
la **fresa** strawberry
frecuentemente frequently

fresco (-a/-os/-as) fresh
frío (-a/-os/-as) cold
fuerte strong
fuerza de voluntad willpower
fumar to smoke
la **función** performance

las **gafas** glasses
la **galleta** biscuit
ganar to earn, to win
la **gasolina** gas
el **gasto** expense
el **gato** cat
generalmente usually
la **gente** people
el **gerente** manager
la **ginebra** gin
las **gracias** thanks
grande big
grave serious, grave
gritar to shout
el **guante** glove
guardar to keep
el **guardia** police officer
la **guerra** war
guisar to cook
gustar to like
el **gusto** pleasure

haber to have
la **habitación** room
hablar to speak, to talk
hacer to do, to make
hacer la maleta to pack (suitcase)
hacia towards
el **hambre** hunger
la **harina** flour
hasta until
el **helado** ice cream
helar to freeze
heredar to inherit
la **herida** injury
la **hermana** sister
el **hermano** brother
la **hija** daughter
el **hijo** son

la **historia** history
hola hello
holgazana (-es/-as) lazy
el **hombre** man
la **hora** hour, time
la **hora de comer** lunchtime
horrible horrible
el **hospital** hospital
el **hotel** hotel
hoy today
hoy día nowadays
el **huevo** egg
huir to run away

la **idea** idea
el **idioma** language
la **iglesia** church
las **ilustraciones** illustrations
importante important
importar to matter
inaugurar to inaugurate
increíble incredible
inglés (inglesa/-es/-as) English
insistir to insist
insoportable unbearable
las **instrucciones** instructions
insultar to insult
inteligente intelligent
intentar to try to
interesante interesting
interesar to interest
el **invierno** winter
invitar to invite
ir to go
ir de compras to go shopping
ir de vacaciones to go on
  vacation
irse to go away
italiano (-a/-os/-as) Italian

jamás never
el **jardín** yard
el **jerez** sherry
joven young
el **jueves** Thursday
el **juez** judge

jugar to play
jugar (a) to play a game
julio July
junio June
juntos together
justo (-a/-os/-as) just

el **kilómetro** kilometer

la(-s) the
el **ladrón** thief, burglar
el **lápiz** pencil
largo (-a/-os/-as) long
la **lástima** pity
lavar to wash
lavarse to wash oneself
la **leche** milk
leer to read
lejos far
lento (-a/-os/-as) slow
levantarse to get up
leve minor
la **ley** law
libre free
el **libro** book
listo (-a/-os/-as) clever
Londres London
los the (plural)
el **lugar** place
el **lunes** Monday
la **luz** light

llamar to call
llamarse to call oneself,
  to be called
la **llave** key
llegar to arrive
lleno (-a/-os/-as) full
llevar to wear, to carry
llevarse to take away
llorar to cry
llover to rain

la **madre** mother
mal badly
la **maleta** suitcase

el **maletero** car trunk
mandar to order
la **manifestación** demonstration
la **mano** hand
la **manzana** apple
mañana tomorrow
el **mapa** map
la **máquina** machine
el **mar** sea
maravillosamente wonderfully
el **marido** husband
el **marisco** seafood
el **martes** Tuesday
marzo March
más more
más tiempo longer
mayo May
la **medianoche** midnight
el **médico** doctor
medio (-a/-os/-as) half
mejor better
mejorar to get better
el **melocotón** peach
menos less
el **mercado** market
el **mes** month
la **mesa** table
meter to put in
mientras while
el **miércoles** Wednesday
mirar to look
mismo (-a/-os/-as) same
mojarse to get wet
molestar to bother, to trouble
el **momento** moment
la **montaña** mountain
montar en bicicleta to ride a
    bicycle
morder to bite
morir, morirse to die
el **motor** engine, motor
mover to move
la **muchacha** girl
el **muchacho** boy
mucho much, a lot

mucho (-a/-os/-as) much, a lot,
    many
muerto (-a/-os/-as) dead
la **mujer** wife, woman
la **multa** fine (penalty)
el **museo** museum
la **música** music
muy very

nada nothing
el **nadador** swimmer
nadie no one, nobody
la **naranja** orange
la **neblina** mist
necesitar to need
negro (-a/-os/-as) black
nevar to snow
ni ... ni neither ... nor
la **niebla** fog
la **nieve** snow
ninguno (-a/-os/-as) none
la **niña** girl
el **niño** boy
el **nombre** name
el **norte** north
la **noticia** news
la **novela** novel
noviembre November
nuevo (-a/-os/-as) new
el **número** number
nunca never

o or
o ... o either ... or
obedecer to obey
la **obra (de teatro)** play
octavo (-a/-os/-as) eighth
octubre October
ocupado (-a/-os/-as) occupied,
    taken, busy
ocuparse de to attend to
ocurrir to happen
odiar to hate
odiarse to hate each other
la **oficina** office
ofrecer to offer

oír to hear
el olor smell
olvidar(se) to forget
el ordenador computer
el oro gold
el otoño autumn
otro (-a/-os/-as) other

la paciencia patience
el padre father
los padres parents
pagar to pay
la palabra word
el pan bread
la panadería bakery
el panecillo bread roll
los pantalones trousers
el paquete package
para for
la parada de autobús bus stop
el paraguas umbrella
parar, pararse to stop
parecer to seem
los parientes relatives
pasado (-a/-os/-as) past, last
pasar to spend (time), to pass
pedir to ask for, to order
pegar to hit
la película film
peligroso (-a/-os/-as) dangerous
la pelota ball
pensar to think
peor worse
pequeño (-a/-os/-as) small, little
perder to lose, to miss (train,
    boat, etc.)
perderse to lose one's way
perdonar to forgive
el periódico newspaper
permitir to allow
pero but
el perro dog
la persona person
pertenecer to belong
el pescado fish (as food)
el pez fish (generic)

el piano piano
el pie foot
la pierna leg
la píldora pill
pintar to paint
el pintor painter
la piscina swimming pool
el piso floor, apartment
el pitillo cigarette
la playa beach
la pluma pen
pobre poor
poco little (amount)
poco (-a/-os/-as) little, few
poder to be able
la policía police
el policía police officer
poner to put
poner la mesa to set the table
ponerse to put on
por by, along
la portezuela car door
la posibilidad possibility
la práctica practice
el precio price
preguntar to ask
el premio prize
preocuparse to worry
preparar to prepare
presentar to introduce
presentarse to appear, turn up
el presidente president
prestar to lend
la prima cousin (female)
la primavera spring (season)
primero (-a/-os/-as) first
el primo cousin (male)
principal main
el principio beginning
probar to try, to test
el problema problem
el profesor teacher
el programa program
prohibir to forbid
prometer to promise
pronto soon

protestante protestant
provocar to provoke
próximo (-a/-os/-as) next
publicado published
el **pueblo** village
la **puerta** door
la **pulsera** bracelet

que what, who, which, that
quedar to remain, to have left
quedarse to stay
quejarse to complain
querer to want, to love
quererse to love each other
quien who, whom
¿quién? who?, whom?
las **quinielas** soccer pools (betting)
quinto (-a/-os/-as) fifth
quitar to take away, remove
quitarse to take off (clothes)
quizá(s) perhaps

rápido (-a/-os/-as) fast
la **razón** reason
razonable reasonable
la **rebaja** reduction
el **recado** message
recibir to receive
recoger to pick up
recordar to remember
el **regalo** present
la **reina** queen
reírse to laugh
el **reloj** watch, clock
la **representación** performance
reservar to book
el **resultado** result
el **retraso** delay
la **revista** magazine
rico (-a/-os/-as) rich, wealthy
el **río** river
el **robo** theft
romper, romperse to break
ronco (-a/-os/-as) hoarse
la **ropa** clothes

roto (-a/-os/-as) broken
el **ruido** noise
ruso (-a/-os/-as) Russian

el **sábado** Saturday
saber to know
saber a to taste of
el **sacrificio** sacrifice
salir to go out
el **salón** living room, lounge
saludar to greet
secar to dry
secarse to dry oneself
seco (-a/-os/-as) dry
la **sed** thirst
la **seda** silk
seguir to follow, to go on
según according to
segundo (-a/-os/-as) second
el **sello** postage stamp
la **semana** week
semejante such
sentarse to sit down
sentirse to feel
las **señas** address
el **señor** sir, Mr., gentleman
la **señora** madam, Mrs., lady
la **señorita** Miss, young lady
septiembre September
séptimo (-a/-os/-as) seventh
ser to be
el **servicio** service
servir to serve
severamente severely
sexto (-a/-os/-as) sixth
siempre always
el **silencio** silence
la **silla** chair
el **sillín** saddle (bicycle)
el **sillón** armchair
simpático (-a/-os/-as) nice, friendly
sin without
el **sitio** place
la **situación** situation
sobrar to have to spare

el **sobre** envelope
sobre on, upon, about
la **sobrina** niece
el **sobrino** nephew
el **sofá** sofa
el **sol** sun
solamente only
el **soldado** soldier
soler to be in the habit of
sólo only
el **sombrero** hat
sonar to sound, to ring
sonreír to smile
soñar to dream
la **sopa** soup
sorprender to surprise
la **sortija** ring
subir to go up, to bring up, to
climb
el **suelo** ground, floor
la **suerte** luck
el **supermercado** supermarket

el **tabaco** tobacco
tal such
la **talla** size
también also
tampoco neither
tanto so much
tanto (-a/-os/-as) so much,
so many
tardar to take time
tarde late
la **tarde** afternoon, evening
la **(tarjeta) postal** postcard
la **taza** cup
el **té** tea
el **teatro** theater
el **telegrama** telegram
telefonear to phone, to call up
el **teléfono** telephone
la **televisión** television
temprano early
tener to have
tener éxito to succeed
el **tenis** tennis

tercero (-a/-os/-as) third
terminar to finish
la **terraza** balcony, terrace
la **tía** aunt
el **tiempo** weather
la **tienda** store
el **tío** uncle
tocar to touch, to play
(an instrument)
todo everything
todo el mundo everybody
todos los días everyday
tomar to take, to have (food,
drink)
la **tónica** tonic water
tonto (-a/-os/-as) silly
la **tortilla** omelette
trabajar to work
el **trabajo** job, work
traducir to translate
traer to bring
tras after (behind)
tratar (de) to try
el **tren** train
el **tribunal** law court
triste sad
triunfar to succeed
el/la **turista** tourist
tronar to thunder

un (-a/-os/-as) a, one, some
la **universidad** university
único only (thing)
usar to use
útil useful
la **uva** grape

las **vacaciones** vacations
vacilar to hesitate
¡**vale!** all right!, OK!
valer to be worth
valer la pena to be worth it
varios (-as) several
la **velocidad** speed
vender to sell
venir to come

la **ventana** window
la **ventanilla** window (of car)
ver to see
el **verano** summer
la **verdad** truth
verdadero (-a/-os/-as) true
verde green
verse to see each other
el **vestido** dress
vestirse to get dressed
viajar to travel
el **viaje** journey
viejo (-a/-os/-as) old
el **viento** wind

el **viernes** Friday
el **vino** wine
el **violín** violin
visitar to visit
vivir to live
volver to return, to go back
la **voz** voice

ya already
ya no no longer

la **zapatería** shoe store
el **zapato** shoe
la **zona** area

English–Spanish

In this section, (*v.*) for verb is next to any English headword that might be read as a noun. The same goes for a few adjectives (*a.*). In the Spanish translations, an asterisk * indicates adjectives that change their form according to gender/number; the masculine singular (or, where appropriate, the masculine plural) is shown.

a un, una
about sobre
accept aceptar
accident accidente
accompany acompañar
according to según
accountant contable
accuse acusar
actor actor
actress actriz
address señas
advise aconsejar
after después (de)
after (= *behind*) tras
afternoon tarde
against contra

airplane avión
airport aeropuerto
allow dejar(se), permitir
all right! ¡vale!
almost casi
along por
a lot mucho*
already ya
also también
always siempre
amount cantidad
amusing divertido
announce anunciar
answer (*v.*) contestar
any alguno*
anything cualquier cosa

apartment piso
aperitif aperitivo
appear presentarse
apple manzana
approach (*v.*) acercarse
April abril
architect arquitecto
area zona
argue discutir
argument discusión
arm brazo
armchair sillón
arrest (*v.*) arrestar
arrive llegar
as como
ask preguntar
ask for pedir
assist asistir
at a
attend asistir
attend to ocuparse de
aunt tía

badly mal
bag bolsa
bakery panadería
balcony terraza
ball pelota
bank banco
bath (*v.*) bañar
bathe (oneself) bañarse
bathroom baño
be ser, estar
be able poder
be missing faltar
be quiet callarse
beach playa
bed cama
bedroom dormitorio
beer cerveza
before ante, antes de
begin empezar
beginning (*n.*) principio
behind detrás (de)
believe creer
belong pertenecer

better mejor
between entre
bicycle bicicleta
big grande*
bill (= *money*) cuenta
birthday cumpleaños
bite (*v.*) morder
black negro*
blame culpa
blind (*a.*) ciego*
blue azul*
boat (= *rowing*) barca
boat (= *ship*) barco
book (*v.*) reservar
book libro
bookkeeper contable
boring aburrido*
bother molestar
bottle botella
box caja
boy muchacho, niño
bracelet pulsera
brandy coñac
bread pan
bread roll panecillo
break romper, romperse
breakfast desayuno
bring traer
bring up subir
broken roto*
brother hermano
build construir
building edificio
bullet bala
burglar ladrón
bus autobús
bus stop parada de autobús
busy concurrido*, ocupado*
but pero
butcher's shop carnicería
buy comprar

call (*v.*) llamar
call oneself llamarse
call up telefonar
cancel cancelar

capital capital
car automóvil, coche
car door portezuela
carry llevar
cat gato
cathedral catedral
celebrate celebrar
censor (v.) censurar
certain cierto
chair silla
change cambio
charge (v.) cobrar
charming encantador*
cheap barato*
check cheque (in a restaurant)
chocolates bombones
choose escoger
church iglesia
cigarette cigarrillo, pitillo
cinema cine
city ciudad
clever listo*
client cliente
climate clima
climb (v.) subir
clock reloj
close (v.) cerrar
clothes ropa
coast costa
coat abrigo
coffee café
coincidence casualidad
cold (a.) frío*
colleague compañero
color color
come venir
come across encontrarse con
come in entrar
companion compañero
complain quejarse
computer ordenador
concert concierto
consent (v.) consentir
conservative conservador
contact contacto
content oneself contentarse

conversation conversación
cook (v.) guisar
cookie galleta
correct correcto*
cost (v.) costar
count (v.) contar
countryside campo
cousin primo (m.), prima (f.)
covered cubierto*
cry (v.) llorar
cup taza
cupboard armario
curiosity curiosidad
custom (= habit) costumbre
customs Aduana

damage daño
dance (v.) bailar
dance, dancing baile
dangerous peligroso*
date fecha
daughter hija
dawn (v.) amanecer
day día
day off día libre
dead muerto*
December diciembre
decide decidir(se)
delay retraso
delicious delicioso*
delighted encantado*
demonstration manifestación
depend depender
describe describir
desk escritorio
die morir, morirse
difficult difícil
difficulty dificultad
diligently diligentemente
dine, have dinner cenar
dining room comedor
dinner cena
director director
disaster desastre
disc disco
dismiss despedir

do hacer
doctor médico
document documento
dog perro
door puerta
doubt (v.) dudar
doubtful dudoso*
drawer cajón
dream (v.) soñar
dress vestido
drink (v.) beber
drink, to have a d. tomar una copa
drink bebida, aperitivo
drive (v.) conducir
drugstore farmacia
dry seco*
dry (v.) secar
dry oneself secarse
during durante

each cada
early temprano
earn ganar
easily fácilmente
easy fácil*
eat comer
edge borde
egg huevo
eighth octavo*
either ... or o ... o
elevator ascensor
employee empleado
end fin
engine motor
English inglés*
enough bastante
enough, to be e. bastar
envelope sobre
error error
evening tarde
everybody todo el mundo
everyday todos los días
everything todo
expect esperar
expense gasto

expensive caro*
explanation explicación

factory fábrica
fairly bastante
fall (season) otoño
fall in love enamorarse
famous famoso*
far lejos
fast rápido*
father padre
fault culpa
February febrero
feel (v.) sentirse
few poco*
fifth quinto*
film película
find (v.) encontrar
find out enterarse
fine (a.) estupendo*
fine (= penalty) multa
finish (v.) acabar, terminar
fire, by the f. al fuego
first primero*
fish (as food) pescado
fish (animal) pez
fit in (v.) caber
floor suelo, piso
flour harina
flower flor
fog niebla
follow seguir
food comida
foot pie
football pools quinielas
for para
forbid prohibir
forget olvidar(se)
forgive perdonar
free libre*
freeze (v.) helar
French francés*
frequently frecuentemente
fresh fresco*
Friday viernes
friend amigo (m.), amiga (f.)

friendly simpático*
from de, desde
full lleno*
funeral entierro
follow seguir
fourth cuarto*

gas gasolina
generous espléndido*
gentleman señor
German alemán*
get angry enfadarse
get better mejorar
get dark anochecer
get dressed vestirse
get married casarse
get tired cansarse
get up levantarse
get wet mojarse
gin ginebra
girl muchacha, chica, niña
give dar
give back devolver
glad, to be g. alegrarse
glasses (= optical) gafas
glove guante
go ir
go away irse
go back volver
go down bajar
go for a walk dar un paseo
go on seguir
go on vacation ir de vacaciones
go out salir
go shopping ir de compras
go to bed acostarse
go to sleep dormirse
go up subir
gold oro
good bueno*
good-bye adiós
goodwill buena intención
grandfather abuelo
grape uva
grave (= serious) grave*
green verde*

greet saludar
ground (floor) suelo

habit costumbre
habit, to be in the h. of soler
half medio*
hand mano
happen ocurrir
happy contento*, feliz*
hat sombrero
hate (v.) odiar
hate each other odiarse
have haber, tener
have (food/drink) tomar
have a good time divertirse
have left quedar
have a rest descansar
have to spare sobrar
hear oír
heat calor
hello hola
help (v.) ayudar
help each other ayudarse
helper ayudante
hesitate vacilar
hill colina
hire (v.) alquilar
history historia
hit (v.) pegar
home casa
hope (v.) esperar
horrible horrible*
horse caballo
hospital hospital
hot caliente*
hotel hotel
hoarse ronco*
hour hora
house casa
how como
how much cuánto
hunger hambre
husband marido
hurry (v.) darse prisa

ice cream helado
idea idea
ill enfermo*
illustration ilustración
important importante*
in a, en
in front delante (de)
in that case entonces
inaugurate inaugurar
incredible increíble*
inherit heredar
injury daño, herida
insist insistir
instructions instrucciones
insult (*v.*) insultar
insurance company compañía de
  seguros
intelligent inteligente*
interest (*v.*) interesar
interesting interesante*
introduce presentar
invite invitar
Italian italiano*

jacket chaqueta
January enero
job trabajo
journey viaje
judge juez
July julio
June junio
just justo*

keep (*v.*) guardar
key llave
kilometer kilómetro
kind amable
kitchen cocina
know conocer, saber

lack (*v.*) faltar
lady señora
language idioma
last (= *past*) pasado*
last (*v.*) durar
late tarde

laugh (*v.*) reírse
law ley
law court tribunal
lazy holgazán*
lean out asomarse
learn aprender
leave behind dejar
leg pierna
lend prestar
less menos
let (*v.*) dejar
letter carta
light luz
like (*v.*) gustar
like como
line fila
listen escuchar
little pequeño*, poco*
little (= *amount*) poco
live (*v.*) vivir
living room salón
London Londres
long largo*
longer más tiempo
look (*v.*) mirar
look after cuidar
look for buscar
lose perder
lose one's way perderse
lounge salón
love (*v.*) querer
love each other quererse
lovely delicioso*
luck suerte
luggage equipaje
lunch comida
lunchtime hora de comer

machine máquina
madam señora
magazine revista
mail correo
main principal*
make hacer
make an effort esforzarse
man hombre

manage conseguir
manager gerente
many muchos*
map mapa
March marzo
market mercado
married casado*
matches cerillas
matter (v.) importar
May mayo
meal comida
meat carne
meet (v.) encontrarse con
message recado
midnight medianoche
milk leche
minor leve*
miss (train, etc.) perder
Miss señorita
mist neblina
moment momento
Monday lunes
money dinero
month mes
more más
mother madre
motor motor
motor coach autocar
mountain montaña
move (v.) mover
Mr. señor
Mrs. señora
much mucho*
museum museo
music música
must deber

name nombre
near cerca
necklace collar
necktie corbata
need (v.) necesitar
neither tampoco
neither ... nor ni ... ni
nephew sobrino
never jamás, nunca

new nuevo*
news noticia
newspaper periódico
next próximo*
nice simpático*
niece sobrina
nightgown camisón
nobody nadie
noise ruido
no longer ya no
none ninguno*
no one nadie
north norte
nothing nada
notice (v.) fijarse en
novel novela
November noviembre
now ahora
nowadays hoy día
number número

obey obedecer
obtain conseguir
occupied ocupado*
October octubre
of de
of course claro
offer (v.) ofrecer
office despacho, oficina
often a menudo
OK vale
old viejo*
omelette tortilla
on sobre
one uno*
only solamente, sólo
only (thing) único
on top of encima
open (v.) abrir
opposite enfrente de
or o
orange naranja
order (v.) mandar, pedir
other otro*
owe deber

pack (*v.*) (*suitcase*) hacer la
   maleta
paint (*v.*) pintar
painter pintor
pants pantalones
parcel paquete
parents padres
parking lot aparcamientoi
party fiesta
pass (*v.*) pasar
past pasado*
patience paciencia
pay (*v.*) pagar
peach melocotón
pen pluma
pencil lápiz
people gente
performance función,
   representación
perhaps acaso, quizás
person persona
photograph fotografía
piano piano
pick up (*v.*) recoger
picture cuadro
pill píldora
pity lástima
place (*n.*) lugar, sitio
play (*theater*) obra (de teatro)
play (*v.*) jugar
play (*an instrument*) tocar
pleasant agradable*
pleased contento*
pleasure gusto
pocket bolsillo
pocketbook bolso
police policía
police officer guardia, policía
poor pobre*
possibility posibilidad
post (= *mail*) correo
postcard (tarjeta) postal
postage stamp sello
practice práctica
prepare preparar
present (*n.*) regalo

president presidente
pretty bonito*
price precio
prize premio
problem problema
promise (*v.*) prometer
protestant protestante
provoke provocar
published publicado*
punish castigar
pupil alumno
purchases compras
put poner
put in meter
put on ponerse

quarter cuarto
queen reina

rain (*v.*) llover
read leer
ready dispuesto*
reason razón
reasonable razonable*
receive recibir
reduction rebaja
relatives parientes
remain quedar
remember acordarse (de),
   recordar
result resultado
return (*v.*) volver, devolver
rich rico*
ride a bike montar en bicicleta
right (= *correct*) correcto*
right (= *direction*) derecho*
ring (*v.*) (*bell, etc.*) sonar
ring (*on finger*) sortija, anillo
river río
road carretera
room cuarto, habitación
row (= *line*) fila
rowboat barca
run away huir
Russian ruso*

sacrifice sacrificio
sad triste
saddle (*on cycle*) sillín
salesperson dependiente, -a
same mismo*
sandwich bocadillo
Saturday sábado
save (*money*) ahorrar
say (*v.*) decir
say good-bye despedirse
school escuela, colegio
sea mar
seafood marisco
season estación
seat asiento
second segundo*
see ver
see each other verse
seem parecer
seize apresar
sell vender
send enviar
September septiembre
serious grave*
serve servir
service servicio
set the table poner la mesa
seventh séptimo*
several varios*
severely severamente
shelf estante
sherry jerez
ship barco
shirt camisa
shoe zapato
shoe store zapatería
shoot (*v.*) disparar
shopping compras
shout (*v.*) gritar
show (*v.*) enseñar
shower ducha
sign (*v.*) firmar
silence silencio
silk seda
silly tonto*
sing cantar

sir señor
sister hermana
sit down sentarse
situation situación
sixth sexto*
size talla
sleep (*v.*) dormir, dormirse
slow lento*
slowly despacio
small pequeño*
smell (*n.*) olor
smile (*v.*) sonreír
smoke (*v.*) fumar
snow nieve
snow (*v.*) nevar
so así (que)
sofa sofá
so many tantos*
so much tanto, tanto*
soldier soldado
some unos, unas
some (= *any*) alguno*
somebody alguien
someone alguien
something algo
sour agrio*
son hijo
soon pronto
Spain España
sound (*v.*) sonar
soup sopa
speak hablar
speed velocidad
spend (*time*) pasar
sport deporte
spring (= *season*) primavera
start (*a car*) arrancar
station estación
stay (*v.*) quedarse
stop (*v.*) parar, pararse
store tienda
straight directamente
strawberry fresa
street calle
strong fuerte*
student estudiante

study (v.) estudiar
stupid estúpido*
succeed tener éxito, triunfar
success éxito
such tal, semejante*
suffice bastar
sugar azúcar
suitcase maleta
summer verano
sun sol
Sunday domingo
supermarket supermercado
surprise (v.) sorprender
sweet dulce*
swimmer nadador
swimming pool piscina

table mesa
take tomar
take away llevarse, quitar
taken ocupado*
take off (clothes) quitarse
take time tardar
talk (v.) hablar
tall alto*
taste of saber a
tea té
teach enseñar
teacher profesor,-a
telegram telegrama
telephone teléfono
telephone (v.) telefonear
television televisión
tennis tenis
tenth décimo*
terrace terraza
test (v.) probar
thanks gracias
that ese*, que
that (= over there) aquel*
the el, los, la, las
theater teatro
theft robo
then entonces
there allí
thief ladrón

thing cosa
third tercero*
thirst sed
this este*
these estos*
think pensar
those esos*
those (= over there) aquellos*
threaten amenazar
thunder (v.) tronar
Thursday jueves
thus así (que)
ticket billete
tie (= neck-) corbata
time hora
tired cansado*
to a
tobacco tabaco
today hoy
together juntos*
tomorrow mañana
too (much) demasiado
touch (v.) tocar
tourist turista
towards hacia
town ciudad
train tren
translate traducir
travel (v.) viajar
travel agent's agencia de
    viajes
tree árbol
trouble (v.) molestar
truck camión
true verdadero*
trunk (of a car) maletero
truth verdad
try probar, tratar (de)
try to intentar
Tuesday martes

ugly feo*
umbrella paraguas
unbearable insoportable*
uncle tío
under bajo

underneath debajo (de)
understand comprender
understand each other
  comprenderse
university universidad
until hasta
upon sobre
upstairs arriba
use (*v.*) usar
useful útil*
usually generalmente

vacations vacaciones
very muy
village pueblo
violin violín
visit (*v.*) visitar
voice voz

wait (*v.*) esperar
waiter camarero
waken despertar
wake up despertarse
walk (*v.*) andar
want (*v.*) desear, querer
war guerra
wardrobe armario
warn avisar
warning (= *sign*) aviso
wash (*v.*) lavar
wash (oneself) lavarse
watch reloj
water agua
way (= *road*) camino
wear (*v.*) llevar
wealthy rico*

weather tiempo
wedding boda
Wednesday miércoles
week semana
well (= *good*) bien
what que
when cuando
where to adonde
which cual, que
while mientras
white blanco*
who que, quien, ¿quién?
whom quien, ¿quién?
wife mujer
willpower fuerza de voluntad
win (*v.*) ganar
wind viento
window ventana
window (*of car*) ventanilla
wine vino
winter invierno
wish (*v.*) desear
with con
without sin
wonderfully maravillosamente
word palabra
work (*v.*) trabajar
work trabajo
worry (*v.*) preocuparse
worth (to be w.) valer
worse peor
write escribir

yard jardin
year año
young joven*

Index

The numbers refer to section headings, *not* pages.